A SHEARWATER BOOK

Halflives

The world of our fathers resides within us. Ten thousand generations or more. A form without history has no power to perpetuate itself. What has no past can have no future. At the core of our life is the history of which it is composed and in that core are no idioms but only the act of knowing and it is this we share in dreams and out.

—Cormac McCarthy, *Cities of the Plains*

BROOKE WILLIAMS

Halflives

RECONCILING WORK AND WILDNESS

ISLAND PRESS / Shearwater Books
Washington, D.C.   Covelo, California

A Shearwater Book
published by Island Press

Copyright © 1999 Brooke Williams

Library of Congress Cataloging-in-Publication Data
Williams, Brooke.
   Halflives : reconciling work and wildness / by Brooke Williams.
     p.   cm.
   Includes bibliographical references and index.
   ISBN 1–55963–577–0 (cloth : alk. paper)
    1. Philosophy of nature. 2. Williams, Brooke. I. Title.
  BD581.W46   1999
  304.2—dc21
                              99–33863
                              CIP

Printed on recycled, acid-free paper

Manufactured in the United States of America
10 9 8 7 6 5 4 3 2 1

To Terry, magic

Contents

Acknowledgments

My thanks go to my father, Rex W. Williams Jr., who seems to get younger with age; soon we will be brothers. And to Shirley, who has made him so happy since my mother has been gone.

To my mother, Rosemary Brandley Williams (April 14, 1932–May 21, 1994)—I found a new, dark world when the ground beneath me collapsed into the void she left. I feel her constantly.

To all my brothers and sisters—Becky and Dave Thomas, Joey and Jann Williams, Nan and Steve Hasler, Tom and Amy Williams, Steve and Ann Tempest, Dan Tempest and Thalo Porter, and Hank Tempest and Marlena Lambert Tempest and to my nieces and nephews, Nate, Abbey, and Libby Thomas; Seth, Adrian, Rosie, and Ben Williams; Cate, Lucy, Sam, and Sophie Williams; Will, Johanna, Jordan, Elizabeth, and Jake Hasler; and Callie, Sara, and Diane Tempest. And our goddaughter Annabelle Milliken.

To John Tempest, who shows me every day that work is life.

To all my traveling companions, both literal and figurative: Glen Lathrop, Scott and Ann Hinckley, Jack Turner, Doug Peacock, Joan Digiorgio, David Mock, Dolores LaChappelle, A. J. Martinez, Chris Noble, Luther Propst, John Shepard, Monica

Woelfel, Creighton King, Barry Lopez, Bob Reiss, Sue Bellagamba, Scott and Melissa Wood, Dan and Bonnie Judd, Bob Helmes, Sandra Lopez, Ron Carlson, Chris Merrill, Gary Nabhan, Nicole Greene, Jeff Foott, Wendy Millet, Tom Till, Larry Clarkson, Rick Bass, Mark and Katie Austin, Tom and Jan Lyon, Bill McKibben and Sue Halpren, John and Anne Milliken, Steve Earl and Lynne Tempest, Bill Kittredge and Annick Smith, Dennis Sizemore and Trent Alvey, Ted and Joan Major, Randall Tolpinrud, Ron Barness, Bill and Eleanor Hedden, Brian Goetz, Catherine Porter, Jenepher Stowell, Dave Bean, and J. D. and Bea Williams, the most solid guides.

To Dave Lovell and Dave Nimkin, always the perfect business partners.

To Lizzie Grossman, Bob Datilla, and Barbara Ras, who provided perfect guidance and support at critical times while I wrote.

To John Fielder at Westcliffe Publishers, Inc., Deb Clow at Northern Lights Publishing, Barry Scholl at *Salt Lake City Magazine,* and Rick Reese at Utah Geographic Series, Inc., who first published different parts of this work in different forms and set valuable examples.

To The Nature Conservancy of Utah, the Southern Utah Wilderness Alliance, the Utah Wilderness Coalition, Round River Conservation Studies, the Wild Utah Forest Campaign, Save Our Canyons, and everyone working to save Utah's wild places.

To Brad Barber, Jeff Burks, Courtland Nelson, Dean Reeder, Sonja Wallace, Suzanne Winters, and all my new friends in state government, the people of the Sonoran Institute, SWCA, and Emery, Wayne, Garfield, Grand, and Summit Counties who make my current work so rewarding.

Thanks to the "Chamber"—the source of all worthwhile ideas.

To Yvon Chouinard, Peter Matthiessen, Jim Harrison, Gary Snyder, and W. S. Merwin, men whom I rarely see but who inspire me daily.

To Paul Shepard, who spent his life reminding us who we really are and the price we pay for not acting that way. Our challenge is to embody his work.

To Jake Burnett, who led me to the petroglyphs that inspired the art used in the text.

I am personally responsible for any soft thinking, speculation, or poor assumptions and any errors in judgment or accuracy. Not Laurie Burnham, my editor, the first I've known to use two pens—black for answers and red for questions. She turned my manuscript into art. I like who I've become during our work together.

And most of my thanks go to my wife, Terry Tempest Williams, who has always known the secret ways and has been unflinching in her efforts to share them with me. Her love fuels me. She is gravity.

Introduction

F IRST, THERE IS THE PICTURE OF OUR PLANET taken through the window of *Apollo 17* on December 7, 1972. Many see the colorful ball, much of it mysteriously shrouded in wispy clouds the length of continents, as proof that we live on a living, breathing organism. For me, the photograph is significant because it is *not* a picture of the world. It is a picture of Earth.

Earth and the world are not the same place. We created the world; it is the map and the globe. Earth is rock and water and tree. Earth would exist without us. The world wouldn't. The world is what we've done to the earth. Lines and borders. Roads and buildings. Pavement, clear-cuts, and mines.

When I read in Paul Shepard's book *Nature and Madness* that "civilization is a veneer," I thought about the photograph of Earth as seen from space, without lines and names. But as I read on, I discovered that Shepard was referring to people:

> Beneath the veneer of civilization, lies . . . the human in us who knows the necessity of a rich nonhuman environment, play at being animals, the discipline of natural history, . . . [and] the cultivation of metaphorical significance of natural phenomena of all

kinds. . . . There is a secret person undamaged in every individual, aware of the validity of these, sensitive to their right moments in our lives.

I believe that this "secret person," this undamaged core, is the root of "biophilia," E. O. Wilson's theory that all humans have an "innate tendency to focus on life and lifelike processes," as explained in his book *Biophilia* (Harvard University Press, 1984). In his introduction to *The Biophilia Hypothesis* (Island Press, 1993), Stephen Kellert writes that biophilia extends our dependence on nature beyond food and other necessities to encompass a "human craving for aesthetic, intellectual, cognitive, and even spiritual meaning and satisfaction."

I can feel that veneer. And I can feel the secret undamaged person in me. In my mind, I see all the protective coverings our culture has developed to buffer us from the elements and keep us safe and special while allowing us to forget where we came from and who we really are. The beauty and value of an orange or a grapefruit are in the rich fruit revealed when the thick covering is peeled away.

One winter, I found an orange in my ski pack that had been there since spring. The peel was brittle. The fruit inside had withered and shrunk to something hard and lifeless the size of a peanut that rattled when I shook it. I wonder whether something similar might happen to us if we forget about the fruit, the core of our lives.

Every year, that veneer gets thicker. More things to buy. More labor-saving devices (pay-at-the-pump gas stations, cellular phones, remote control everything) freeing up time so we can work harder to earn enough to afford all the things we need to help us save time. Our happiness depends on how thick that veneer is, the degree to which civilization covers our lives. Or so we're told. Economic growth is the only way our culture knows to measure success.

And as the world prospers, the earth suffers.

My former job was all about money. How much I made depended on what else I was willing to sacrifice. But I was unchallenged. I couldn't see where what I did made any difference. If I weren't doing my job, someone else would be. I made up for my malaise by buying things I could stand back and admire, thinking, *What a great job I have. Look at all the great things I have.* A new car every other year. The latest skis and bikes. Fancy dinners with customers. Season's tickets. But it couldn't last.

Now, on the surface, my life seems out of control. Everything takes too much time. The garage overflows with things I don't care about but don't have time to move. Our yard is on its way back to its "precolonial" state. The siding on the house is falling off and needs painting. I rationalize my lack of attentiveness by insisting that these details are of the world and not the earth. Yes, my veneer is a mess.

One day, while trying to understand an engineer's drawing, I got out an old physics book. I came across a diagram of a backpacker climbing a hill, illustrating "work." In physics, work is force multiplied by distance. I had carried many packs up many hills, but no one ever called it work. Certainly not my father, my grandfathers, and my great-grandfathers, who all put work in a special category at the top of their lives, next to church and family. I made a copy of that page and kept it; the image became a metaphor for me. Real work means applying a force to an object and moving it over a distance. It is effort and movement. My real work was applying the force of my own muscles to the object (my own body) and moving it over the vast distances of the Tetons, Yellowstone, southern Utah, Montana, Alaska. In my job, I applied plenty of effort, but nothing ever moved.

I grew up with the story that associated work with subduing nature and subduing nature with success: land cleared for new homes, spreading higher on the hillsides every year; new ski areas. As children, we measured growth and progress and how well the family business was doing by the view from our home on the hill above Salt Lake City: the spread of the copper mine across the valley, the number of downtown buildings higher than the Mormon temple. When not subduing nature, we either ignored it or admired it from a distance, like a painting in an art gallery. Or we feared it for its potential to cause floods, fires, earthquakes, or droughts that threatened to harm what we'd earned with our hard work.

When I was eighteen, I discovered a new, wild story, one where I felt more alive in nature than I did in town. Nature was no longer an opposing force to overcome. I loved its soft and rounded surfaces, I loved exploring red rock deserts, running rocky trails, and skiing deep powder. I wanted to know every-thing about the earth—how it worked, what came from what, and why. I wanted to know how my own body worked, and why.

I spent years testing which story was mine. Then I spent years struggling to navigate between the two, between wildness and work. I wanted to be part of wild nature, but I knew I needed work and culture to survive. I was living two completely separate halflives: a responsible half I could design and control and a wild half I couldn't. I thought that living any other way was impossible in modern society.

I was in college when I got my first taste of a complete life. At the time, half of my life was schoolwork and church and sum-mer jobs and half of it was running and climbing and skiing and discovering how wild things all made sense. This revelation came to me while I was in Nevada doing research on wild horses for my senior biology project.

We'd been out five days, and I hadn't seen a single horse. No matter. Our project didn't require actually seeing any. The point was to test out whether domestic cattle and wild horses were competing for forage; if they were, the ranchers could lobby to have all the horses removed from the range. Our plan went like this: We divided the desert according to slope angle. There were four categories—very steep (more than thirty degrees), steep (fifteen to thirty degrees), sloped (less than fifteen degrees), and flat. My partner would carry a six-foot pole in a straight line for one hundred paces across the desert. I would follow, counting the horse droppings and cow pies that fell beneath the stick and recording the information in a notebook. Then we would trade. Back at school, we would analyze the data, looking for evidence of "niche overlap." A lot of cow pies and horse droppings in the same transect would indicate competition; little overlap would show that the ranchers' fears were unfounded.

That afternoon, when the others were taking a break, I wandered off to explore. Five minutes later, I came to the edge of the arroyo.

The scene was as perfect as I'd dreamed it: a dozen all-colored mares, three brown colts and one wild stallion, black and shiny as obsidian, spread out below me, drinking from a small stream. I dropped to my belly, mesmerized.

Somehow, minutes or hours don't work to measure time in situations like that. Measuring by the depth of the holes small rocks made in my elbows, the taste of my dry tongue, or the darker color of the air, I watched the black stallion for a long time. He noticed me the moment I lay down, glaring with eyes so fiery angry that I found it difficult to look back. He was huge and strong, and the light coming in at that low evening angle cast shadows along the huge muscles in his shoulders. His tail touched the ground.

I'd read that most wild horses are just a generation or two from being tame, offspring of ranch stock who escaped from some nearby corral. Some, however, have the wild blood of the horses ridden by Hernando Cortés and other Spanish conquistadores as they plundered the region while looking for gold five hundred years ago. It's said that one can tell the Spanish horses by the zebralike stripes on the backs of their hind legs.

I searched the legs of every horse for stripes but couldn't find any. But whether the horses had recently escaped or were descendants of a more ancient lineage didn't matter. These animals had escaped from the saddle and picked wild over tame. They were surviving—thriving, as near as I could tell—on their own wits, going their own way, guided not by some bridle but by something older and deeper, from the middle of their cells. Something wild that their former owner thought he could breed or train away.

I quietly rolled over, grabbed my notebook and pencil, and started recording the scene: numbers, colors, time of day. Suddenly, an inner voice warned me that I had become too focused on my notes and had let my attention lapse. I jerked around to see that the stallion was gone. I turned. Somehow he had climbed the embankment soundlessly and reached the trees ten yards below, stalking me from behind. I'd read tales of cowboys killed, stomped to ground level, by mad stallions. I leaped from my perch and sprinted upstream. Pounding hooves shook the ground behind me and branches broke; a scream reverberated from the center of the earth. I turned to see the stallion rise

on his hind legs, his front legs clawing the air. With a magnificent midair pirouette, he raced back to his family and led them
away like the wind.

I stood there, gasping because I'd forgotten to breathe. My
heart pounded, and I could taste fear in my mouth. I bent over
and leaned on my knees and wanted to throw up, and I had to
pee. But I couldn't move.

My project lost its significance after that wild stallion chased
me. I felt euphoric, high, as I gathered my books and pens that
had scattered when I ran. Although some daylight remained, I
couldn't work any more. My classmates and I had been living in
our own world, a small world we'd made up ourselves: a series
of desert patches, one hundred steps long and six feet wide. For
five days, that world had been all there was. Then, in less than
a minute, that world exploded when a wild force erupted in the
shape of a wild, black horse. In that moment, my halflives
emerged, then merged, giving rise to a feeling that was almost
chemical or electric, like a dream, in which bizarre and impossible things are normal and accessible. Something brand-new
formed: a different, albeit temporary, life. When the sensation
faded, I desperately wanted it back.

I'd felt my wild side stirring even before my encounter with the
stallion. I owe part of my awakening to Scott Hinckley, a friend
from high school, where we played football together. He played
tackle; I was the fullback. Otherwise, we didn't have much in
common. Hink was big and strong and quiet and spent his free
time hunting or hiking. Back then, I was more social and had little interest in outdoor activities, probably due to past negative
experiences as a Boy Scout. Hink and I became close in college,

when most of our friends were off serving their missions for the Mormon Church.

It was the same every week: Hink and I and whoever wanted to come bolted from class early Friday afternoon to spend Saturday and most of Sunday hiking and camping in the mountains or the desert. Then we would shift feelings as if they were giant psychic gears, slowing down, easing into the dread of a whole week of sitting and thinking. Getting back to Salt Lake City in the wee hours of Monday, we would find ourselves propped up in a 7:45 class, after never enough sleep. We devoted our lives to getting away, moving, balancing the long, bitter bouts of sitting in class or the library with the sweetness of prolonged natural contact. Although I didn't know it at the time, part of the experience was doing biological experiments on what would become the most fascinating organism of all, my own body.

We both majored in biology: Hink as part of his pre-veterinary courses and me because I loved wondering about nature and uncovering clues to how life's pieces fit together. I had no idea where biology would lead me; still, I never expected the wild horse project to turn me upside down.

That trip was different from all the others. For the first time, a camping trip to the desert wasn't an escape from college; it was part of it. We had a *full* week. And we got credit.

But that trip was monumental for another reason. I saw for the first time a glimpse of a complete life, one that wasn't divided into halves struggling against each other. I still believe that life has two sides—that each of us is an amalgam of nature and culture, wildness and work. Our challenge is to find the right mix, the balance, and the courage to make the necessary adjustments.

PART I

Blood

Knowing the story of your people in gossipy detail means you're nearer to placing yourself in relationship to what is called the blood of things.

—William Kittredge, *Hole in the Sky*

One

I COME FROM A LONG LINE OF HARD WORKERS, all Mormons. "Put your shoulder to the wheel; push along." These words were drilled into me every Sunday. I knew that if it weren't for unflinching faith and hard, dirty, knuckle-breaking work, our ancestors never would have made it to Utah.

Nor would the Great Salt Lake Valley have "blossomed like a rose." When Brigham Young and his 149 followers arrived in 1847, the place was a desert. Although totally exhausted from a hellish four-month journey, they couldn't rest. They began immediately to create their own world to insulate themselves from the earth. In two days, they had dammed and diverted City Creek to irrigate large plots, where they planted beans, buckwheat, turnips, corn, and potatoes. Within a week, they had built a road to haul wood from a nearby canyon, set up a blacksmith shop, and sent an army of hunters and fishermen to find meat. By the seventh day, Brigham Young had chosen a site for their temple and laid out plans for a city of 135 one-acre blocks. Sprouting corn had turned three acres bright green. Within three weeks, this bedraggled group of settlers had built twenty-nine houses.

One hundred fifty years later, nearly a million people live in the Salt Lake Valley, people who have never stopped working. The beehive, an icon of industry, stands as the official symbol of Mormonism. Freeways are constantly being torn up and widened. New office buildings seem to appear overnight, many of them furnished with equipment my family has always made their living by selling. Two blocks from my office, a new assembly hall is being built because the old one, on Temple Square, is too small. Stonecutters will decimate the cliffs south of the city to quarry enough granite for a four-inch-thick veneer to match the original six-foot cubes that form the walls of the Salt Lake Temple. Before the roof went on, the building looked like the Parthenon.

I grew up with the frantic feeling that I needed to get out and go as far and hard as I could because in a few years I would be tamed by the "real world." I would get married, have children, work all week at the family business, then go to church on Sunday. I didn't even need to think about it; that future seemed real enough to have been programmed in my cells. To anyone who knew our family, it was.

As far as I can tell, I am the first in my immediate family to consider breaking up the small compartments where we keep the different parts of our lives. Work and church both have their own "rooms," with alarms that go off to remind us when to move from one to the other. Play is in a room with everything that is not in the work room or the church room. Although my whole family loves the natural world, I sense that they don't see themselves as the integral part of it that I do. I think that for them, the natural world is kept in the miscellaneous room, with play.

In my family, the work room and the church room are adjoined. From the time I was a small child, the only work I knew was selling for Rex W. Williams & Sons, Manufacturers'

Representatives. My great-grandfather, Thomas Allen (T. A.) Williams, was the first manufacturers' representative west of the Mississippi. He sold saddles, nails, coal chutes, and rope out of his small office in the Dooley Building in downtown Salt Lake City. The building was torn down to make room for a hotel.

T. A.'s son Rex, my grandfather, went to work for him in the 1930s, after stints in the army and as a park ranger at Yellowstone National Park. People who know me and knew my grandfather say I look like him, which makes me proud. He branched out on his own, adding building supplies—copper pipe, floor and roof drains, toilet partitions, flush valves, and shower equipment—to his inventory. Rex and his wife, Helen, had three boys, Bob, J. D., and Rex Jr., my father.

Pictures of those men in my family express the formality of a new generation, eager to show that it has succeeded in buffering itself from the need to find or raise its own food and build its own shelter. This new generation wears suits every day while creating wealth from more modern, indirect sources, not as creators, but as organizers and information disseminators. Not from the land reacting to the length of day, the season, and the moon phase, but at a desk putting words and numbers on paper that has become the new and necessary link that connects producer to consumer in a new world where they no longer need to know each other. A suit says "I no longer work with my hands." In the photographs, this new generation is proud of its stout veneer, proud to be building a brand new world that for the first time in history is totally separate from the earth. I get the feeling that my grandfather's generation not only ignored its human core, but defied it, or thought they'd extinguished it.

My grandfather was the perfect gentleman. I can count on one hand the number of times I saw him without a tie. I saw him get angry only once—when I flippantly mentioned that I might not stay in the family business. "The men in your family have worked through hard times to keep this business going," he said. "There is no more honorable task a father can perform than to pass on a good reputation and a very decent livelihood to his sons."

I can't imagine him ever being a young man. To him, work, church, and family were all that mattered

My grandfather mastered the art of keeping his lives separate. During one period, he kept an office in the basement of the family home. "He never brought his work upstairs," my father recalls. "He rarely spoke of his work, and as young boys, our only exposure to it was while traveling with him on summer sales trips."

My grandfather spent any free time fishing and watching television, especially sports. He and I may look alike, but I did not inherit my love of movement from him. As far as I know, his main form of exercise was walking from the car to the fishing hole. After he underwent coronary bypass surgery at age seventy-two, his doctor insisted that he ride his new Exercycle five miles every week while he watched television. My grandfather knew that the doctor would be dropping by every week to check the bike's odometer. Not about to change his lifelong habits, he kept special candy for the grandkid who could ride the fastest mile when we came to visit every Sunday. When Grandpa hit seventy-five, the doctor said he could quit exercising.

My father, Rex Jr., attended the University of Utah, majoring in mechanical engineering and graduating about the time my older sister, Becky, was born. Instead of joining Rex W. Williams & Sons, he moved with my mother and their baby to Albuquerque, New Mexico, where he had a job designing missiles and bombs for the Sandia Corporation. I was born the next year.

It's not clear whether my parents were just homesick or whether the frustration of my father's major project—a bomb that was designed to detonate after burying itself underground but instead kept exploding on impact—was too much, or both, but after two years, we moved back to Salt Lake City.

My father's oldest brother, Bob, was already working for the family business; his older brother, J. D., never considered it. J. D. had been interested in politics since serving as president of his junior high school. He was motivated academically and adventurous enough to leave Utah for Stanford University and then Harvard. He returned with a Ph.D. degree and took a job teaching political science at the University of Utah, where he taught for forty years. Throughout his life, J. D. has paved the way for me to be different. By his example, he showed me that many alternatives to the family business existed and that good work could add real passion to one's life. When he retired, eleven parties were held throughout the city because so many people wanted to honor him. For months afterward, people were spotted all over town wearing red, white, and blue buttons printed with the words "J. D. Taught Me." J. D. taught *me* that there is more to work than making money.

For technical and personal reasons, my grandfather decided to split Rex W. Williams & Sons into separate divisions in 1968. Uncle Bob took over the architectural specialties—lockers, toilet partitions, and washroom accessories. My father was responsible for the plumbing—flush valves, shower equipment, and drains. Rex Sr. presided over both divisions until he turned seventy and sold his shares to his sons. He continued to work for the company, preparing bids and providing technical support. A customer once told me that if I could ever learn as much as "Senior" had forgotten, I would be doing well. He finally retired at age eighty-four, a few months before he died.

My father and his brother Bob butted heads at work, mainly because their styles were so different. Bob belonged to every professional organization and believed that going to dozens of monthly meetings was the most effective way to promote the business. He did most of his actual selling by entertaining customers at the Ambassador Club downtown. He was a lovable man with a huge heart and a gregarious personality who always took care of people needing help. He was full of ideas and was always promoting new products, but I think he had difficulty with the day-to-day details.

In contrast, my father is much more down-to-earth. He works hard all day, every day, his only distraction being tennis instead of lunch on Wednesdays. He and I always said that although ours was not the most interesting profession, it allowed us the time and money to do the things we were passionate about. The family business has allowed my father to provide for his family while giving him the freedom to do his church work.

Unable to mesh their different styles, Dad and Uncle Bob decided to turn their divisions into separate companies. Several years later, in 1975, Bob died of a massive heart attack, alone in a hotel room in San Francisco. He was only fifty-six years old.

According to a prearranged agreement, my dad ended up with both companies, and Maxine, Bob's widow, received a cash settlement. At this point, with my father responsible for twice the work and Bob gone, my path in life seemed clear.

Two

I F FOUR GENERATIONS IN THE PLUMBING INDUSTRY seem deep, they are—but not when compared with my Mormon roots. Looking back, I'm not sure which lineage had the stronger pull in my life because they both tugged in the same direction.

Lucy Decker, the second of Brigham Young's twenty-six wives, arrived in the Great Salt Lake Valley two years after the first Mormon settlers. Her youngest child, Clarissa (we call her Clicky), was my great-grandmother, making Brigham Young my great-great-grandfather. I've done some quick arithmetic. Lucy Decker had six children, and Clarissa had five. If all of Brigham's twenty-six wives averaged four kids, who each had four who had four, and so on, I would have 6,656 special cousins.

In her book *Brigham Young at Home,* Clarissa (Young) Spencer referred to her father and what he had accomplished when she wrote, "Do I praise too highly when I call such courage and vision, magnificent?"

A photograph of my great-great-grandfather hangs prominently in our living room. He is sitting in a chair with his right arm resting on a wooden table, his top hat beside him. In this picture, he looks like a man who could frighten children, as if he could see into their souls and read all their thoughts. When I was growing up, this was the image I saw when I thought of Brigham Young, and I felt guilty every time I looked at it.

In 1994, a new statue of Brigham Young was installed in the rotunda of the Utah State Capitol Building, and now when I think of him, this statue is what I see. He is younger, in his mid-forties, I think. He is mid-step in a confident stride, carrying a stout stick in his left hand. His legs are like trees, and he is wearing high boots. His eyes gaze off to the left, as if he is thinking. His hair is swept back; the wind might be blowing. This statue is full of hope and the possibility for everything he would do or dream in his life. This statue is nine feet tall. Life-sized.

Every week when I was growing up, my brothers and sisters and I went to Sunday school at the ward house. Where we lived, these Mormon Churches were spaced every mile or so. Two or three wards, or neighborhood groups of one hundred families, met at staggered times throughout the day every Sunday. Were it not for the steeples, these modern brick buildings would look more like schools. Each meeting started with singing and praying, followed by two "two-and-a-half-minute" talks, which were intended to inspire but also to train young people to speak in front of large groups. Every child was expected to give these talks from the age of three or four. I still remember some that I gave. There was one about a sprinter who had been burned in a fire but still won races and another about a professional golfer who was ridiculed because he refused wine at a party but went on to win the tournament the next day because everyone else had become sick from the wine. I think my favorite was about a poor boy who lived on one side of a wide valley. Every evening, he would look east across the valley and see a house with beautiful golden windows. He vowed that someday he would live in a house like that. Finally, he couldn't stand it any longer and set out across the valley to find the house. But he arrived at the other side of the valley after dark and had to wait until morning to continue his search. When the sun came up, he couldn't find the house with golden windows. Discouraged, he turned toward home. As he looked west across the valley, he saw, to his astonishment, that his own house now had golden windows.

My mother was the only one who made her children memorize their talks. When we were young, she would make us practice with her while she ironed. In addition to insisting that we have all the words down, she made sure that we talked slower than seemed normal and enunciated each word.

At sacrament meetings, we heard announcements about new assignments for members and who was sick and needed extra prayers. The sacrament was blessed and passed, and then talented ward members sang solos or played violin. Visiting church officials or new members gave talks. I always took notepaper to write down what I was thinking. My dad carried trick eyeglasses with wide-open eyes painted on the lenses so no one would be able to tell he was napping during the hour-and-a-half meeting. I never saw him use them, although we knew they were in his pocket.

Usually, the talks were too complicated for children and I think that sacrament meeting was more training to sit for long periods on hard benches and for being together as a family. I busied myself by playing pencil games like hangman, sending secret signals to my friends across the chapel, making cartoon flipbooks out of the hymnal, and establishing records for the amount of time I could keep the sacrament bread from dissolving in my mouth. I remember most of the talks my father gave. He always used colorful personal stories to illustrate his points and somehow managed to engage the entire congregation.

I remember one talk given by someone other than my father. The subject was "natural man" and I was fairly young when I heard it. Our house had a wild field behind it where I spent every daylight hour playing during the summer. To me, nature was flowers no one had planted or needed to take care of, and beautiful bugs and birds. Nature was peace and motion. The speaker confused me when he referred to the word "natural" in a negative way. He read scriptures that would be some of the first I highlighted when I was given my new leather-bound scriptures. He read section 67 in the Doctrine and Covenants, verse 10, " . . . you shall see me and know that I am not with the carnal neither natural mind, but with the spiritual." I thought it might just be a Mormon idea until he read from the New Testament, 1 Corinthians 2:14: "But the natural man receiveth not the things of the Spirit of God; for they are foolishness unto him." I remember thinking that if God made nature, how could the "things of the Spirit of God" be foolishness to the Natural Man? The division between spirit and nature just didn't make sense.

When I turned eighteen, talk turned to a mission. I wasn't shy about telling anyone who asked that I didn't want to go, which carried the same social implications as dodging the draft. The bishop and I had many private conversations in his office, although I don't remember specific details. Every Sunday, when he saw me in the hall between meetings, he'd say, "Come on, Brooke, let's take the long walk." Once, a wealthy neighbor who owned an egg company offered to pay for my mission, as if my reluctance were a matter of money, with my father not wanting to pay for it, which was far from the truth.

Most Mormon parents view their son's mission as a major step not only in his spiritual advancement but also toward a responsible adulthood. In fact, the mission seems designed to prepare young men for corporate America as much as to expand the church. Women who have not married by the time they are twenty-one are encouraged to go on missions. Missionaries have a rigid schedule that includes early morning scripture study; ten to twelve hours of door to door proselytizing from Monday through noon on Saturday, "P Day"; preparation and recreation on Saturday afternoon; and meetings and public worship on Sunday. Goal setting and an emphasis on results are important elements. The number of "discussions" or lessons the missionaries teach each day and the number of people they convert or baptize matters. Distractions, especially involving women, are to be avoided. No matter where in the world they serve, missionaries are to have short-cropped hair and wear dark suits, ties, and white shirts. Loyalty, commitment, and discipline are implicit in the missionary model, a model that might also describe young IBM middle managers.

In 1970, it was crystal clear to everyone that I would not be going on a mission. My lottery number came up as forty-five, indicating that I could be drafted into the armed services and would likely end up in Vietnam. My family hoped that the idea of getting a religious deferment by going on a mission might bring me to my senses. But even with the Vietnam War looming, the price seemed too high. Two years in a tie teaching something I wasn't sure I believed seemed distant and dark, like a new kind of death. I know my father was disappointed when I told him I just couldn't go. But he was always supportive. I know he struggled, realizing that pushing me too hard might push me away too far.

Fortunately, he had other children with no such qualms. I joke with him about his still owing me my share of the thousands of dollars he spent to send my brothers and sister on their missions. He laughs, saying, "Sorry, you had your chance." Joe and Tom went to New Zealand and St. Croix (in the Virgin Islands), respectively. Nan went to Germany. They all came back with faith-promoting stories, but I don't remember the specifics. What I do remember is a photograph of Joe skiing in New Zealand in his dark suit, his tie flapping in the breeze. "We only took one run," he said when I asked him if skiing was against the rules.

In the end, I avoided Vietnam by joining the Army Reserve and agreeing to six months of basic training followed by one weekend of active service each month for six years. Although I hated basic training, I still think back to four things that happened to me during those months: I learned how to cut off a man's head silently, using a coiled piano wire; I became acutely aware of how much I missed the Wasatch Range above my home in Utah; during hand-to-hand combat training, my opponent from Chicago told me that we'd get killed on his neighborhood streets using the techniques we were being taught ("Believing what they tell us is more important than what they tell us—they're training us in blind obedience," he said); and I discovered that Sundays did not have to be spent in church. For the first time in my life, I had Sundays off. I went for long walks, wrote letters, and read antiwar novels. During one telephone conversation with my father, he suggested trying out the army ward. I thought about going to church but chose not to. My own time to reflect about the Vietnam War and be with new friends who would be leaving and might not return seemed more important.

As soon as I returned from basic training, I enrolled in college. I was eager to learn, especially about the way the earth worked. Hink and I teamed up to spend long weekends in any wild place within eight hours' drive of home: The Tetons. Cataract Canyon. Salt Creek. Slot canyons in Zion National Park and along the Escalante River. Powder skiing in the Wasatch. Being in the wild became more spiritual than recreational. It was like learning a new language or finding balance. Looking back, this period marked the birth of my halflives.

During week- and month-long biology field trips, I learned to look beyond beauty to the reason for beauty: the cat's-eye marks on the moth's wings stare upward to scare off birds; petals marked with ultraviolet pathways guide insects into the private parts of plants; the raw brilliance of the male mallard's green head and the bull elk's antlers are irresistible to females; the flower of the long-throated scarlet gilia is designed to fit a hummingbird's bill.

In geology, I learned how time and pressure had compressed old oceans and sand into distinct rock layers to form the Colorado Plateau and how the process took billions of years.

Not seven days, as I'd learned in Sunday school. In fact, I am mystified by those who believe that biological evolution and the vast dimensions of geologic time are at odds with the divine. To me, nothing could be more miraculous or provide better evidence of the existence of God. Chapter 88 in the *Doctrine and Covenants,* one of the standard works of the Mormon Church, describes the majesty of the natural world:

> The earth rolls upon her wings, and the sun giveth
> his light by day and the moon giveth her light by
> night, and the stars also give their light, as they roll

upon their wings in their glory, in the midst of the power of God. Unto what shall I liken these kingdoms that ye may understand? Behold, all these are kingdoms, and any man who hath seen any or the least of these hath seen God moving in his majesty and power. (Verses 45–47)

I have experienced this. I believe it.

Three

TERRY AND I MET AT SAM WELLER'S BOOKS, a bookstore in Salt Lake City where she worked. She and my little sister, Nan, were sorority sisters. Nan had been telling me about Terry for months, this woman who loved nature as much as I did. I thought she was too young. She was nineteen; I had recently graduated from college. We met the day after I returned from a month-long river trip. I was starved for reading material, and Weller's was the best bookstore in town. I was with my beautiful girlfriend, Norv. Terry was ringing up our purchases when she overheard us talking.

"My goal is to own the entire set," I said to Norv, pointing to the shelf of Peterson Field Guides.

Norv didn't say anything, but Terry did.

"I have them all," she said, without looking up from her work.

When Terry saw my name on my check, she turned red. Nan had obviously been talking to Terry about me, too.

That was November.

Things didn't work out with Norv. When she told me it was over, she said she was leaving me for Art, not as in a man named Art but as in drawing and painting, which is what she was studying in college.

Terry and I played a few games in order to see each other, while trying not to seem interested. I needed a book for a Christmas present, so I had her take it home, where I picked it up, meeting her family at the same time. In turn, she brought her mother and grandmother into the ski shop where I worked, under the guise of looking for a jacket for one of her brothers.

"That is who Terry will marry," her mother said on their way back to the car.

Friends from high school invited Norv and me to a New Year's Eve party, but since Norv would be spending the holiday with Art, I needed a date. On a whim, I called Terry a few hours before the party, and to my surprise she agreed to go.

We talked all night. I was smitten.

Later, two friends who had been at the party called, wanting to know how serious I was about Terry. They both asked if they could take her out. I said, "Hell, no."

Besides one week I spent ski touring in Yellowstone and another camping alone in Arches National Park assessing the situation, Terry and I were inseparable for the next five months. Every week we went skiing and bird-watching at the Bear River Migratory Bird Refuge. Terry took a botany class in the spring quarter, and we spent every afternoon in the foothills with hand lenses, keying spring beauties, glacier lilies, and various vetches.

I quickly found out how spiritual she was and how much Mormonism meant to her. Even so, we fell profoundly in love, in the fairy-tale sense. I vowed to be what I had to be to be with her. I would even be a Mormon. My parents were ecstatic, thinking that Terry was my salvation, an answer at last to their prayers and to all my hard questions.

God, we were happy. We talked about getting married in the fall, when she returned from Jackson Hole, Wyoming, where she was to spend the summer at the Teton Science School, and after I had finished a season as a boatman on the Colorado River.

On May 1, Terry called me with the news that the Teton Science School was looking for an instructor to replace one who'd just quit. She asked whether I would be interested.

"I'll need to think about it," I said.

"They need to know in the next few days," she replied.

"OK. I've thought about it. Yes, I'm interested."

It became immediately clear that neither her parents nor mine were comfortable with our going to Wyoming, where we would basically be living together. The solution was simple: we would get married.

Terry's dad took it hard. After missing him twice, I finally caught up with him at half past six one morning in his office at his construction company, to ask for his daughter's hand. His door was open, and he was sitting at his desk, jotting down notes. "John," I said. He looked up from his work.

"We're not hiring," he said.

Because Terry wanted it more than I didn't, I agreed to a temple marriage. We went through the prescribed steps to show our worthiness—I stopped drinking the occasional beer and we avoided sex, at least the prohibited kind. After interviews with our bishops and stake presidents, we got our recommend, the pass that proved we were worthy to enter the temple.

The temple was intense. A few days before our wedding, we went to the Provo Temple to take out our endowments, the first step in the process that would end on our wedding day, when we would be sealed together, not "until death do you part," but "for time and all eternity." Temple sealing is a prerequisite for entry into the Celestial Kingdom. The endowment consisted of sitting in a room with a hundred other people, men on one side and women on the other, watching live theater depicting the ritual of life acted out by temple workers. They were all dressed in white except for the devil, who appeared in a black business suit. There were three rooms, one for each kingdom. Adam and Eve and the snake were there, and the eating of the fruit. The endowment ended when all the Adams (the men) led all the Eves (the women) through a veil to a beautiful room representing eternity.

Those who have completed their own endowments are encouraged to go back to the temple often and do the endowments and sealings on behalf of people who have died without being able to do it for themselves, which is most of the world. Determining who all those people are is a huge job, so the church expends enormous effort on genealogy.

All the wards have a night every month on which members get together and go to the temple. Now the church is building smaller temples all over the world and especially in rural Utah so that people living in Monticello and American Fork don't have to travel far to do endowments. Hopefully there are enough faithful members going to enough temples to do endowments for everyone who ever died. I understand that there are old people who go every day. Members of other religions have expressed concern over Mormons' performance of these rituals on behalf of their dead relatives, which is understandable. The quick answer for these critics is that those in the next life have the opportunity to accept or reject the endowment.

"It reminded me of the Hopi," I remember saying when Terry and I left the temple after our first ceremony.

A few weeks earlier, I had read Frank Waters's *Book of the Hopi,* a beautiful description of the sacred and ritualized lives of Native American people, and wondered why we modern white

Americans have avoided sacredness and ritual in our lives. After our endowments, I realized that we have our own.

Terry and I were married on the morning of June 2, 1975. All members of our immediate families and our best friends were there—about three dozen people. Those with recommends were inside the temple with us; those without waited on the temple grounds. I felt sad that Terry's grandparents, Mimi and Jack Tempest, weren't inside. Sanky and Lettie Dixon, her other grandparents, were, though rumor had it that in order to get a recommend, Sanky had been subjected to delicate negotiations involving a commitment to coach his ward's softball team and a discount on bats at the sporting goods store where he worked part-time.

We were sealed (married) while kneeling on an altar in a room surrounded by chairs filled with family and close friends. The walls were mirrors, and when I looked over Terry's shoulder as we knelt, there were a million of us, stretching off forever.

After a big wedding reception complete with swans carved in ice and a new brown suit, we left for a four-month honeymoon of teaching and working at the Teton Science School.

Once we had settled into life in the Tetons, we were too busy or too tired for church. We promised each other that we would find a ward as soon as we moved back to Utah. I considered the Teton Science School a place I was simply passing through on my way from youth to adulthood. I seriously believed that having a wife, a house, a church, and a job would curb my desire for wild places and wild things.

When we returned to Salt Lake City and found a house to move into, we didn't have to look hard for the Mormon Church. The bishop and one of his councilors showed up while we were still opening boxes, happy to hear that we were members. They told us the meeting schedule and asked us about our interests. They also asked me where I had served my mission.

"The Wind Rivers, Escalante," I replied. "The Colorado River Mission." (Hink and I had always joked about being on our "missions" when we were exploring.)

They looked puzzled but continued on, asking whether we needed anything. I had them help move some furniture, even though I knew that physical labor wasn't what they'd meant.

From the beginning, we were responsible church members. I taught Sunday school to twelve-year-olds, and Terry worked with the young women. The bishop could feel that our hearts weren't in it, and he tried to keep us active in the church by keeping us busy. As time went on, I felt less motivated and more frustrated. I found myself dreading church on Sundays and started to feel a deep, slow pain growing every Saturday night. The pain was similar to what I felt on Sunday night in anticipation of work on Monday. I knew what it felt like to be truly alive, and this wasn't it. My brain was fighting my body.

Terry was changing, too. I think she had once assumed that Mormonism was the basis for her intense spirituality, but she was learning that the two forces were separate. We tried hard to be good church members for a few years. We really did. Then we began spending more weekends away.

Together, we had more courage to follow our own path. Although I knew I was butting heads with family history, I felt comfortable pulling away from the church. I knew that Joseph Smith had had his Sacred Grove, and I had mine.

About that time, we moved into a new neighborhood. We never looked for the ward, and the ward never looked for us.

Four

O UR WORK AT THE TETON SCIENCE SCHOOL ended on October 2, our four-month anniversary. It was time for me to get on with my life. If I followed in my father's footsteps, who had followed in his father's, who had followed in his father's, my job at Rex W. Williams & Sons would be the last I would ever have. I'd had my fun; it was time to settle down. I had chosen my other jobs, all temporary, with my halflives in mind. I had been a ranger in Zion National Park, by night patrolling roads and campgrounds and by day, on my own time, exploring intimate canyons formed by massive sandstone walls and filled with maidenhair ferns and icy pools. In another job, for a year I had hiked, biked, or skied up a closed canyon to collect water samples. I'd worked at an outdoor gear shop that offered a generous employee discount. And Terry and I had just finished an incredible honeymoon working and teaching at the Teton Science School.

My office was in the back of a converted tile shop on Fourth Avenue, across the street from the city cemetery. It was a strange one-story building with huge windows in front framed by elaborate tiles. Near the top, the words *Rex W. Williams & Sons* were displayed in blue metal letters, with two huge wrought iron chandeliers hanging from chains at each end of the company name. The company sells equipment for commercial construction, but because of the building's unique design and its proximity to the cemetery, many people assumed that our business had something to do with death. Weekly, grief-stricken relatives of the recently departed would come in inquiring about gravestones or burial vaults.

I inherited Uncle Bob's office, which was pretty nondescript. His desk, which sat against one wall, was wooden and huge and came with a soft leather chair with wheels and worn-out arms. If I got too relaxed, the chair would roll across the sloped floor to the center of the room. The desk was empty except for the long center drawer. Lois White, who had been the company secretary for twenty-five years, had filled it with notepaper, pens, a stapler, and a phone finder with every number I might need. There was a plastic-wrapped box containing business cards with my name engraved at the bottom in beautiful black lettering. Behind me, gray metal shelves stored twelve neatly aligned catalogs, one from each of the manufacturers we represented.

All manufacturing companies need salespeople. Big companies have full-time sales forces. Smaller companies hire independent companies such as Rex Williams & Sons, who represent numerous noncompeting manufacturers, pay their own expenses, budget their time, and are paid a commission on everything they sell. Inside many of the catalogs on my shelves were personal notes from vice presidents and sales managers who had become family friends over the years.

My office had no windows. I hung a framed photograph of the Tetons on the one existing hook. Years later, I would be in that office when the space shuttle *Challenger* blew up.

I arrived for my first day of work dressed uncomfortably but appropriately—in a wide striped tie with a crooked knot, the best I could do; a checked sport coat; and matching blue pants that would not wrinkle. I had a beard left over from my time in the Tetons. I kept it for five years, constantly aware that in our business, beards symbolized a radical character. I finally shaved it off one night after having dinner with the vice president of one of the companies we represented. I'd taken the afternoon off to ski, barely making it back in time for dinner. In the middle of an important discussion, a big twig had fallen out of my beard and onto the white tablecloth.

I spent until noon that first day shell-shocked, sitting with the door closed, feeling small and overwhelmed. I wondered if sitting there with a tie around my neck signaled the end of my wild halflife. Periodically, I checked my legs to see if my thigh muscles had softened.

From that vantage, I had two choices: I could make it work, or I could stuff my new jacket and tie into the crack under the door and wait to suffocate. I seesawed between the two thoughts until lunchtime.

After lunch, I pulled the blue Bradley catalog off the shelf. The Bradley Corporation makes the gang showers found in almost every high school locker room. The company also manufactures wash fountains—the big round or half-round stone basins that, when you see one for the first time, you don't know whether to pee in it or wash in it, or both. Studying the catalog reminded me that Bradley also makes stainless steel accessories such as toilet paper and paper towel holders for public rest rooms as well as urine specimen cabinets and combination cabinets for hospitals. The company also makes vandal-proof prison fixtures, such as a weird sink with a toilet sticking out the side. A nice note welcoming me to the industry from Tom

Brown, Bradley's sales manager, was clipped to the catalog. I'd met Tom once before, when he came to town and took our whole family out to dinner. He and I would become friends; he would come skiing and backpacking with me and send me articles on environmental issues he thought would interest me. He died in his mid-fifties, of a heart attack while jogging. Many of his colleagues wondered how the stress of traveling and corporate life might have contributed to his death.

I recognized all the equipment in the catalogs. My brothers and sisters and I had grown up with these things. I remembered the stainless steel sinks with built-in faucets. Somehow, all 158 of them installed in St. Mark's Hospital had dispensed cold water when the handle pointed to *H,* and vice versa. As one of the dozens of projects my father arranged for us to do to raise ski money, we took apart every faucet and switched the mechanism—just as we'd cut 5,000 round filters out of square ones, put 80 new latches on urine specimen cabinets, installed new handles on thousands of lockers, and riveted number pins to every locker key at the Deseret Gym. "The company figures it will take one minute to fix each one. I know you kids can do it faster than that," my father always said. Usually, we could.

Before five o'clock that first afternoon, I studied the catalogs for Sloan flush valves, Zurn drains, and Corning glass pipe products. I left the toilet partitions, lockers, and washroom accessories for the next day.

Five

A T FIRST, TERRY AND I LIVED IN A RENTED COTTAGE with a nice yard that our landlord took care of. When we moved in, fresh from the Teton Science School, we were shocked to find that all houses didn't come with toilet paper, garbage cans, cleaning products, and plants. We spent all the money we had on Clorox and Kleenex and not a dime on outdoor gear. Even so, my wild halflife stayed relatively healthy; I still spent evenings and weekends outside. My work side was different. Although my job helped provide the means to live the life we had chosen, work itself was a void, totally detached from wildness.

At Rex W. Williams & Sons, I was involved with the products we represented at every stage of a construction project, from the design stage to the time the building's owner assumes responsibility for them, a year after the building is finished.

The West High School gym is a good example. Eight months before the scheduled bid date, I read in the *Intermountain Contractor,* a weekly construction magazine, that the Salt Lake City School District was planning the new gym. The magazine has all the important information about every construction project: architect, engineer, schedules, etc. I knew the engineer because we'd done many projects together. When I called him, I already knew what the job might require: showers, faucets, flush valves. I knew he would want our gang showers, the kind with five or six heads coming from the top of a column. We agreed to meet to discuss shower systems, but mainly to share our latest powder skiing adventures. When I went to see him, I tried to interest him in using a new thermostatic valve on all the showers. I explained that the device prevented scalding by incorporating a strip made of two different metals laminated together and wound into a coil. If for some reason the cold water flowing to the valve were reduced or shut off altogether, the hot water would cause the coil to flex, moving a slider to close down the hot-water port and balancing the temperature of the water coming out of the shower head. I showed him a sample. He wasn't convinced that the valve was worth the extra cost, but he said he wanted to try it in the coach's shower room. He wanted a specification describing the valve to include with the mechanical plans going out to prospective contractors. I faxed it to him later that day.

A month later, the gym was out for bid. We knew it was because every day, my youngest brother, Tom, and all the other equipment suppliers and subcontractors went to the plan room maintained by the publisher of the *Intermountain Contractor,* where blueprints for all pending projects are kept. For the school gym project, Tom put together a quotation on all the equipment we sold for the wholesalers, who marked it up with their profit, added prices for other products they sold, and gave it to the mechanical contractors the day before the bid opening. The mechanical contractor added up all the equipment—the fixtures, the boilers, the valves, even the pipe and the sand to bury the pipe, everything. Then he added all the time he estimated it would take to construct and install the mechanical system. He gave that price to the general contractor, who added it in with bids from all the other subcontractors and submitted his price at the formal bid opening. The school district opened all the bids and eventually awarded the job to the general contractor with the lowest bid. Ideally, that contractor would have ended up working with the low mechanical bidder, who would have given all the fixture orders to the low wholesaler. But chances are that there were some shenanigans with prices on this job because of its large size.

Eventually, after some negotiations, promises, a lunch or two, and maybe tickets to a basketball game, we got the order for all the showers. We submitted shop drawings so the contractor would know how to install them. We ordered the quantities the plans called for. Before the showers arrived at the job site, we talked to factory representatives probably twenty times about their dimensions, their scheduled shipping dates, and why we had sold them so cheaply.

School started before the job was completely finished. One morning, I got a call from the wholesaler, who had been called by the mechanical contractor, who had been told by the engineer that one of the new thermostatic valves in the coach's shower room wasn't functioning properly—no hot water. The valve was on the punch list, which contains all the items that don't work or meet specifications. Not until all items on the punch list pass final inspection does the contractor get final payment for the job. It's my job to get the products I sell to work right.

"If you get right over, you might be able to fix it before she comes in," the wholesaler told me.

"She?" I asked.

"Yes. It's in room 10B, Women's Coach."

I had on a suit and tie for a presentation I was to make to a group of architects later that day, but I decided not to change; this job would be quick. Luckily, there was a window in room 10B; I'd need the dim light it admitted into the room because the electric lights wouldn't work without a key. Although it was dark inside the shower, I knew that valve inside and out. I could fix it in my sleep, and if I could fix it in my sleep, I could certainly fix it in the dark. With the wholesaler's description of the problem, I already knew that the valve needed a new slider.

I brought in the tool kit I kept in my Jeep, and in a second I had popped the escutcheon plate, exposing the raw valve. Using my screwdriver, I closed off the "cold" stop, cutting off the flow of cold water to the valve body. Then I screwed in the "hot" stop. Something didn't feel right. It turned but didn't seem to tighten. I turned it farther and then figured it must be all right.

I had to take out three screws to expose the valve guts and the problem. I had two of them out and was working on the third when the valve exploded, hitting me in the tie. The guts, propelled by twenty gallons per minute of 120-degree water, were all over the floor, which was filling up with water. My shirt and tie were soaked.

I had a couple of choices. I could find the main valve some-where in the building, but I was already standing in four inches of water and a long search didn't seem like an option. The only thing to do was fix the stop. I did the most logical thing I could think of: I stripped down to nothing and hung my clothes beyond the reach of the rising water.

Naked, I climbed back in the shower, holding my screw-driver in one hand and using the other to deflect the hot water.

The water was rising above my ankles as I felt my way to the stop and inserted the tool, applied all my weight, and felt it catch as it turned. In a moment, the water stopped. The world was suddenly calm. I felt around and found the missing pieces and replaced the slider. Then I got dressed. I didn't know what to do with the water, but it was slowly draining away, and what the hell, the floor was tile.

I met the coach at the door. I guess she couldn't think quickly enough to ask what a guy in a soggy suit was doing in the women's locker room. I told her I was sorry about all the water.

Visiting wholesalers was my lifeblood. They actually bought the products. I liked calling on most of them; we'd chat and catch up on each other's lives, even though friendly relationships never really translated into more business. When it came time to order, loyalty didn't matter; the only salesman most of them cared about was the one with the lowest price. Most wholesalers also blamed me for things I had no control over—lost or late shipments, defective products. On really bad days, I would get calls from angry wholesalers who believed that the more abusive they got, the quicker would be the response, a strategy that probably works more often than not. But not with me. "I don't get paid enough to listen to this," I said more than a few times.

On good days, I would make money for the company, spending my time either floating between customers and making new friends or working in my office, where I could always find time to scour maps for my next wild adventure. All too often, I would get depressed about my life cycle of working all one day to pay for shelter and food to keep me alive just so I could do it all again the next.

For the first year of our marriage, while she was finishing college, Terry continued working at Sam Weller's and brought home books instead of money. One day, she surprised me with a used set of the manuscript edition of John Muir's journals. Glued inside the cover of the first volume was a section of Muir's actual journal. He had written his entries in ink and edited them in pencil. These were from notes he'd taken in 1879 while traveling in Alaska to study glaciers.

I read Muir's handwriting about Alaska every day for a month, and then we made plans to go there ourselves. My college friend Hink had married Annie, his childhood sweetheart, and they were living in Anchorage. Hink worked as a veterinarian during the week and explored the vast Alaskan wilderness on weekends.

"You want a month for vacation?" my father asked when I told him about Alaska. "I've never taken a month off in my life."

"Maybe you should try it," I said.

Terry graduated from the University of Utah and found work teaching at a private school. We bought a bungalow with a fence and a mortgage and an orange couch on an easy payment plan, and we went to church most Sundays. From the outside looking in, our lives were in order; by all outward signs, we were a successful young couple. Inwardly, though, I had a struggle going on like a storm between my ribs. On one side, the world was telling me that our car and house were not big or new enough, the sound from our stereo not what it could be. With enough hard work, I could do better. On the other, my body was telling me I had only one need: to be out in wild country. That need held onto me like gravity.

All I could think of were days off, secret canyons to explore, deep powder to ski. I panicked, afraid I would get old and look back to see that I'd followed the same well-worn (paved) path everyone else had. I couldn't do it. But I didn't know the way out. I started running at night, first to be stronger for longer trips on shorter time frames, but then because, somehow, darkness is its own wilderness.

Growing up, I'd watched my father spend most of every Saturday moving through a list of house projects—cleaning back rooms, building shelves, fixing faucets, moving furniture, painting, washing cars, organizing tools, doing yard work. I don't know what I'd been thinking. Maybe I thought all houses came complete with a man like my father.

Although I did manage to mow the grass once in a while, I will never understand our culture's obsession with weeds, why we pull and kill the plants that want to be there just to encourage those that obviously don't.

To my mind, relaxation and recreation are, respectively, passive and active ways not to work. I came up with this definition while watching my co-workers and customers. To them, television viewing, poker playing, reading, and spectator sports were forms of relaxation. Active sports such as skiing, softball, volleyball, and hiking were recreation. Most of my colleagues also categorized bowling, golfing, and fishing as recreation, but I'll risk an argument by slotting these in a gray area between the two. Exercise fit in neither category. No one I worked with did any.

Although I enjoy sports on television and watching movies, I don't spend a lot of time relaxing in that way. I prefer to devote my "not-working" time to recreation. Most people recreate to feel new and less mentally weary, to move their muscles and give their brains a break. But isn't a main goal of recreation to get more and better-quality work from us, to make us more efficient at our jobs? The word *recreation* doesn't accurately explain what I feel at the end of an eight-hour, thirty-mile hike and run in the Uinta Mountains or during the five-minute gut check before a hundred-foot rappel out of Behunin Canyon in the dark, nor does it explain my exhilaration after a week of living in a sandstone cave. Not recreation but creation: life itself.

Six

YEARS AGO, I DREAMED ABOUT ALBUQUERQUE. More specifically, I dreamed about the house where I lived for the first year of my life. My mother, my sister Becky, and some friends from Salt Lake City were playing with me. My father was not in the dream. He must have been at work, designing bombs. In my dream, I look just as I do in an old family photograph, a picture that makes everyone who sees it laugh. I'm in a red wagon, and Becky is pulling me. My head is huge, like a pumpkin; everyone wonders how on earth my mother gave birth to me. (Terry thinks that, on an unconscious level, this photograph made her too scared to want children.) In my dream, my mother is happy; she is the beautiful young woman in her high school yearbook whose photograph I stared at. The dream haunts me because all the time we were growing up, I don't remember many occasions when my mother expressed happiness.

My dream about Albuquerque was important because before then, my painful memories went back further than my happy ones, which began when I was six or seven. Maybe there is a place inside us where our experiences are stored not by value (good or bad, positive or negative) but by time and significance. I remember what happened to me this morning, but most such memories are "soft" and dissolve quickly without being saved. Yet there always seems to be room for significant experiences, even if that storage place needs to expand to hold them. I remember a car wreck that happened when I was three or four. We had one car in those early years in Salt Lake City, and my mother had loaded us in to pick up my father from work. Somehow the car ran off the road, and then rolled over when my mother overcorrected. Miraculously, no one was seriously hurt. I do remember the huge purple-and-yellow bruise on my mother's leg, and I remember seeing the smashed car and wondering why we had lived and thinking about what if we hadn't. I also remember the summer day when I killed our pet rooster and chicken. I had forgotten to move their box out of the sun, and they died of heat stroke. Why do I remember the Little League games we lost more clearly than those we won? And why do I remember being sent to my room on numerous occasions for bad behavior and temper tantrums when I cannot so easily recall my mother's hugs? Once I wrote a running-away note in red ink on the inside cover of my *Fun with Chemistry* book, though I never did run away.

I have vivid memories of my mother's anger, most of which was directed at me. I've agonized over this, not selfishly, over the way her anger affected me (I deny that it still does), but over what caused her anger and why later in life it completely left her. And now those early memories sit alongside newer but no less vivid ones of her intense affection and support.

I know she had a skewed vision of perfection and made it her goal: Perfect Mormon wife and mother. Perfect meals, perfect house (our living room had plastic paths across it that came up when guests arrived). And perfect children. I'm sure I rarely measured up.

My mother, Rosemary, was the last of seven daughters born to Harold and Elsie Talmage Brandley. In 1936, before the advent of antibiotics, her mother died of strep throat. Rosemary was only four years old. Elsie, daughter of James E. Talmage, a Mormon scholar and the author of some of the religion's most powerful works, had been distinguished in her own right. At the time of her death, she was among the church's elite women, holding many important positions, including the presidency of the General Relief Society. She also wrote a column called "Hello Life" for the *Deseret News,* a church-owned newspaper that is still one of Salt Lake City's two dailies. In 1930, her columns were compiled into a book by the same name. Terry and I collect copies we find in used book stores. Elsie and my father's mother, Helen Spencer Williams, were lifelong best friends and their children spent time together.

Three months after Elsie's death, Harold summoned his daughters and told them to get dressed up because he was going to the train station to pick up someone special. My mother remembers waiting with her sisters for what seemed like hours until they heard the front door open. With their father was a woman none of them had ever seen before. "I want you to meet Georgeanne," their father said, "my new wife." Georgeanne was from back east, was about the same age their mother had been when she died, and seemed friendly enough. Harold had picked her up at the train station, but the two hadn't come directly home. Apparently he had called my other grandfather, Rex, from the train station and asked him to call the ward bishop because he was getting married. Rex, realizing that he couldn't reason with Harold, made the arrangements, and an impromptu wedding was held. My father was seven years old at the time and doesn't remember any of it.

Georgeanne, a stalwart Mormon, had read Elsie's work in

the *Church News,* a section of the *Deseret News* that is sent to church members all over the world. The two women had corresponded for a few months, and when Elsie died, Georgeanne began writing the newly widowed Harold a series of letters. Although she had her own children, she offered to come west and care for his family. The depths to which Harold had sunk following his wife's death can be measured only in the level of irrationality required for him to marry a woman the same day he met her.

The details are sketchy because those who knew wouldn't say much about it, but from the beginning, Georgeanne took a real dislike to my mother. Possibly Georgeanne saw young Rosemary as the apple of Harold's eye and became jealous of the young girl. Or perhaps she simply lacked interest in raising a young child. What is clear is that Georgeanne horribly mistreated my mother, mentally more than physically. Harold and her older sisters met all of Rosie's physical needs, but those spaces only a mother can fill stayed empty. Georgeanne criticized everything my mother did and killed any confidence that might have survived Elsie's death. I am convinced that the loneliness my mother suffered, the failure, and the loss—all at such a young age—chipped away at her heart. While growing up, my father was continually told to "take care of Rosie."

The contrasts between my two sets of grandparents were striking. Grandpa and Grandma Williams lived in a lively house full of light and laughter and had endless basement rooms full of old and interesting things (chests, scrapbooks, tools, board games my father had played as a child). I was sure that no one but my cousins and me ever entered those rooms; they were ours to explore. In full view on the grand piano was a statue of the most beautiful woman in the world dancing naked on a golden ball, her arms outstretched. We were sure that our grandparents had left it out by mistake, so we hid in order to sneak looks at it. When their house was sold after they died and everything was given away, Terry and I chose that statue. Now it sits on a bookshelf in our home.

Grandpa Brandley and Georgeanne lived in a small, dark apartment, a scary place for young children, but we visited them dutifully every Sunday all the same. My grandfather spent most of his time in his basement shop, where he cut and polished and mounted stones he'd found to create beautiful jewelry. He also did all the cooking. Georgeanne had Tina, a mousy, barky Mexican Chihuahua dog with a raspy voice. Grandpa and Georgeanne both complained a lot—mostly about liberals and the government. Every Christmas, a miniature holiday village took over the front room. Georgeanne put a fence around it—to protect it from the dog, she said—but we knew it was there to keep us out.

I took Terry to meet them soon after we met. Grandpa and Georgeanne loved Terry, who always finds the best parts of people, and they both brightened when she was around. The four of us even went places together, Georgeanne carrying Tina in one arm, with a leather purse that opened and closed like an animal trap hung from the other. Her fingernails were long and dirty, and her eyes always looked off to the side.

Two weeks before Terry and I were married, Grandpa Brandley asked me to follow him downstairs. He had something to show me. He was making earrings for Terry out of tiger eyes, beautiful brown stones that he said came from petrified asbestos. Then he told me how important sex is to marriage. He told me not only where to touch Terry but also exactly how and why and for how long. I'd never seen him so tender, and I still think about his eyes not moving from the stone he was polishing.

In 1980, when Grandpa Brandley died at age eighty-one, Georgeanne went to Texas to live with one of her own children. We aren't sure, but we think she took a lot of our family history with her. We do know that James E. Talmage's journals and other significant memorabilia were missing when we cleaned out their apartment. We didn't hear much more about Georgeanne until she died, years later. But her death convinced me that she had been obsessed with what she knew about Elsie. I believe that Georgeanne came to Utah to become Elsie Talmage Brandley. When she died, her daughter wrote to us saying that Georgeanne had been ready to "go." She'd cleaned out her room and organized her things and even had written her own obituary. A copy was enclosed. We were shocked to find how similar Georgeanne's obituary was to the one that had been published when my grandmother, Elsie, died nearly fifty years earlier. Only the name and dates had been changed.

Nine and a half months after marrying my father, my mother gave birth to her first child, Becky. I was born ten months later. By the time she was twenty-five, she had had four children. She was thirty when Tom, her last child, was born. From a parent's perspective, perhaps the one good thing about having five closely spaced children is that they leave home almost all at once. Within four years, we'd all gone but Tom, leaving huge amounts of space in the house and in our parents' lives. Still in their forties, they began a new chapter. They redecorated their house and bought a condominium in St. George, a sunny little town in southern Utah. And they spent three years in Tampa, Florida, where my father presided over the Mormon mission.

My mother took up quilting. She loved fitting together scraps of colorful material to form intricate patterns, like a puzzle. Wherever we traveled, Terry and I looked for unique fabrics to take home to her. My brothers and sisters and I all have quilted pillows and wall hangings in our homes, and all the grandbabies were given quilts to keep them warm. And every year, my mother contributed a quilt to an auction to raise money for a hospital.

I remember watching the Escher-style birds on one of her quilts seemingly change directions when I moved from one side of the room to another. And the quilt we hung in the funeral home near her casket had a hundred small, three-dimensional boxes that turned in the light. Once, Becky's husband, Dave, asked Mother if she would make a quilt for his new office. He wanted to pay her, but she wouldn't let him. She couldn't, she said. If she did, she would learn how little her time was worth, something she didn't want to know.

When she died, each of the children picked a quilt from her room. Terry and I chose one she hadn't finished. The completed top piece was neatly folded in a plastic box with the batting and the bottom sheet. Two years later, Terry wanted to surprise me at Christmas. She called Mormon Handicraft, a store where quilters buy their needles and such, to get the name of the best quilter in town. When she called, the woman said she was too busy getting ready for Christmas and, with six young children, simply didn't have the time. Then Terry told her about my mother and the quilt she hadn't been able to finish before her death. The woman agreed just to see the quilt. When she saw the quality of the stitching and the beautiful pattern—

linked framelike squares in different shades of green—she had to finish it. She told us afterward:

> It was so strange. I felt your mother's hand guiding mine. I wasn't sure about the border. I didn't know what pattern to use. Then, one night I had a dream and saw the chain stitch I would use. When I finished, I folded up the quilt and put it back in the box. I noticed a piece of paper folded in the bottom. It was a note your mother had written, with a pattern for the quilt stitching. To my amazement, it was exactly the pattern I'd used. Her hand *was* guiding mine.

My mother's last quilt is so beautiful that we might have framed it and hung it on our wall, but we didn't. We spread it over our bed, and we sleep under it every night.

PART II

Bone

This other speaks of bones, blood-wet
And limber, the rock in bodies.

—Jim Harrison, *Fairboy/Christian Takes a Break*

Seven

THE COMPANY BOUGHT ME A NEW CHAIR for my desk. Although it was lighter than Uncle Bob's and not as apt to roll downhill, I found that I still could not sit for extended periods. Finally, I stopped blaming my chair and accepted the fact that I just don't sit well. I'm sure that spending an hour and a half on a church bench every Sunday for most of my life caused me irreparable psychological damage; to this day, that is the time span by which I gauge my sitting. Fortunately, my job had flexibility, and after an hour of sitting at the desk while writing reports or bidding on jobs, I could justify wandering out to the warehouse or driving off to visit customers.

One day, while reading the *Wall Street Journal,* I came across an article titled "The Hazards of Sitting Down on the Job." The author, Nathan Edelson, made the point that our bipedal species is not equipped for sitting; hence the problem of finding a comfortable office chair. Edelson wrote, "We human beings evolved over the past 250,000 years as animals that must move frequently to maintain adequate lubrication of joints and to keep muscles from getting stiff." Sitting bothers us because our bodies were not meant to sit. We were meant to move.

The article inspired me to think about human evolution.

Throughout most of our history, we've lived as hunters and gatherers, moving from place to place and eating plants and animals that were evolving along with us. Then, as recently as 10,000 years ago, we abandoned that nomadic lifestyle in favor of agriculture. The outcome was culture and civilization and life as we now know it. But the wheels of evolution turn slowly, and our physical evolution has not kept pace with cultural evolution and the rise of civilization in our lives. Our bodies were designed for a world vastly different from the one we're living in. How can we compensate?

Steven Simms teaches anthropology at Utah State University in Logan, an hour's drive north of Salt Lake City. I attended a lecture and slide show he gave about a massive archaeological site along the shores of Great Salt Lake. He and his students discovered the site while looking for prehistoric ceramic pieces and arrow points exposed by the lake's receding waters. To everyone's surprise, one of the students found the lower jaw of a human skull protruding from the sand. No one had been expecting to find bones.

When the Northwestern Band of the Shoshoni Nation decided that the bones of their relatives were no longer safe from looters, they allowed archaeologists to excavate seventy-seven skeletons and store them at Utah State. Although the human bones and skulls in the slides Dr. Simms showed were old and decayed, they looked exactly the same as those in the skeletons I'd studied in human anatomy class. The only difference was time: the skeletons in anatomy class had belonged to modern humans; the bones in the slides came from ancients. Something about the photographs made me shudder. I wanted to know more about the bones and the Fremont people they had belonged to. I called Simms the next day to ask a few questions, and he asked me whether I wanted to see the bones. Yes, I did.

I usually tried to make the ninety-mile trip to Logan every few months to visit with wholesalers and update them on current product information and pricing. Since the wholesalers there didn't get much attention, they were happy to see me. I could justify spending the whole day in Logan, so I left my office early. Besides the running gear and hiking boots that were always stashed in the back, my Jeep was loaded with catalog sheets with new products and price lists and some samples, including a new gold-plated flush valve that no one would ever buy but everyone liked to look at.

Methodically, I stopped to visit the three local wholesalers to say hello and update my catalogs. I listened to them talk about one another and made notes about complaints and orders that needed expediting. Ordinarily, I would have hung around and made small talk for a while, but on this day I was on a mission: I had an appointment with Simms. I hoped like hell that none of the wholesalers would have a project I needed to visit or an architect with a problem. They didn't, and I was finished by two o'clock.

Six shelves sit against one wall of the anthropology laboratory at Utah State, each holding five brown cardboard boxes the size of orange crates. The boxes contain human bones. Steven Simms climbs a stool, carefully removes the box labeled 42Wb48-3, and hands it to me.

Simms is quick and tight; and I think he must be a runner or a bicycle racer. He steps down and leads me into another room, where I set the box on a large table. We have not spoken since we entered the laboratory. He opens the box, and I look in at a pile of brown bones. The room fills with some of that same wild feeling I get watching coyotes hunt or hearing elk bugle in the fall. I do not know how to act around those bones.

A skull, *just like mine,* I think to myself, stares up at me with deep holes that once held eyes. Simms reaches in with both hands and carefully lifts the skull out of the box, holding it for a moment before passing it to me. There are two jagged holes through the top and something that looks like erosion on the forehead. "She had cancer," he says quietly.

I hold the skull while Simms examines other bones. It is very quiet in the room. Every bone in the box looks as if it has been eaten from the inside. Simms looks around as if to see if anyone else might hear what he is about to say. "She was in horrible pain when she died," he says, as if he had been there, as if he had known her. I stared into the absence of her eyes.

Simms whispers when he talks of the bodies in anything but purely scientific terms because he knows that to his colleagues and most anthropologists, those bones belong in a category referred to as "other," different from modern humans. Simms refuses to see them that way. He refuses to see differences between people—between hunter-gatherers and farmers, between Fremont and Desert Archaic cultures, between the living and the dead. Between us and them.

The Fremont were possibly the last Americans to live by hunting and gathering, a lifestyle going back to the beginning of human time, back to our apelike ancestors living in trees in East Africa. The Fremont lived in the marshes at the edge of Great Salt Lake in A.D. 600–1500.

I try to imagine my own ancestors in Europe. The Crusades take place, the Magna Carta is signed, and the first medical school is established. A man wearing eyeglasses reads a book printed with movable type. At the same time, in North America, in a place that would one day be called Utah, Fremont people are eating pine nuts and bulrush seeds, repairing cracked ceramic vessels with stone drills, and playing games using pieces of polished bone. Breathing underwater through a reed snorkle, a Fremont man waits for the duck decoys he has made from twisted twigs to lure mallards; in Europe, Leonardo da Vinci sketches flying machines.

I leave Logan and drive directly to the site where Simms told me the Fremont remains had been found. The weather is spring, trying to be hot. I park at the end of the pavement and walk along a levee built to separate a freshwater bay from Great Salt Lake. Knifelike boats cut the water just for the fun of speed; people read and sun themselves. Ropes of white-faced ibis loop out over the marshes. A fisherman yells at his wife, and I almost trip over a dead, dog-sized carp lying in a pile of his own scales. Marshes still affected by the rise and fall of the lake stretch to the left. I find a way through the thistles and tamarisk that cover the dry side of the levee. There are too many cans for me even to begin picking them up, and a small area is paved with broken glass.

Then I step through a wall of cattails and the world fills with buzzing. Blackbirds—red-winged and yellow-headed—sing their watery songs. Nondescript ducks in eclipsed plumage take flight. Brine flies cover my clothes, and something bites me; I can feel its poison in my arm. A snowy egret fishes in the distance. I see the same world the Fremont woman had seen with her own long-gone eyes, and I wonder what happened to her way of living. I remember something Simms said in his office: "Origins are irrelevant in evolution. There is only movement. . . . There is no such thing as an event, only process.

"Other," he said, "is us."

Eight

I AM NOT A HUNTER AND HAVE "HUNTED" only once. Years ago, in Nevada, I hunted rabbits with a friend. He wounded a large cottontail, and unable to watch it suffer, I grabbed the gun and shot it through the eye. We skinned and cooked it and ate it as a sacrament. I am not interested in killing. I am interested in how hunting has always connected humans with the nonhuman world.

I know from reading Paul Shepard that hunting is what most men have done from the beginning of human time, until ten thousand years ago, when we took up farming. In primitive societies, hunting is embedded in custom, ritual, and story. Hunting forges deep obligations, people to people and people to the gods. It weaves a bond between the hunter and the wild landscape so pure and complete that the line where one ends and the other begins is invisible.

Modern mass hunting is more about managing wild ungulates in an era void of predators. For most modern "hunters," hunting is not about the huge piece of life that death is, the meaning and significance of animals, or how big, rich, and infinitely complex the world is. Rather, the activity has been transformed into weekend extravaganzas of beer and gluttony and guns and gut piles and fat people having heart attacks. It is about killing.

I never went hunting with Hink, but I know that he, his father, and brothers were serious hunters and spent days looking for the right animal to shoot. Sometimes they came home empty-handed, but it didn't seem to matter. The stories were enough—the huge bull elk they didn't shoot because the terrain was too rugged to get him out, though they claimed "he could have made Boone and Crockett." Or all the times they didn't shoot because of distance and not wanting to hit a leg and lose the animal, who would likely have died a painful death. Hink's considerable dissection skills in the biology lab came from all the animals he'd cleaned and butchered. He often gave us meat. It all tasted good because Hink always took care of the animals he killed, but I liked moose the best.

Once, while looking at a spectacular wildlife calendar, I was stunned by how close the animals appeared, by the details of their habitat, by their eyes. It occurred to me that although wildlife photography is not hunting, it might be closer to what hunting used to be than what it is now. One of the pictures in this calendar, depicting a sea otter, had been taken off the coast of California. I read on the bottom of the page that the photographer was Jeff Foott from Jackson Hole, Wyoming. I called Jeff to ask him whether or not he saw similarities between primitive hunting and wildlife photography.

"I've never thought about it," he said.

He talked for a minute about getting to know his subject and trying to "crawl into an animal's skin" to get pictures of behavior no one had ever seen before. Then he agreed with me that the killing—the pull of the trigger, the release of the spear or bowstring, and then the eating—are the visible elements of hunting. Less obvious are the stalking, learning, listening, and waiting. Jeff believed that these are the parts of hunting that are like photography.

Jeff seemed to like my questions, so I asked if I could watch him work sometime.

"I'll be in Idaho looking for bears," he said, "then in Montana photographing slime molds, and then, by the end of the month, in Washington finishing my killer whale film. Take your pick."

"Slime molds?"

"There are no good slime mold pictures."

"I'll meet you for killer whales," I said. I needed to go to Washington anyway for a sales seminar, and I could add on a few vacation days.

Between whale breaths, the water west of San Juan Island's southern tip seems solid. It is smooth and dark, the green shade just shy of black. I imagine stepping out of the boat onto a firm surface and walking off across the sea like some modern-day Jesus. I reach over the gunwale and am surprised to find no resistance as I dip my hand into Puget Sound. I am waiting for a pod of ten killer whales to surface for their third of three breaths before sounding, diving for five minutes of salmon fishing.

Until this morning, I was sure I'd jinxed the trip. I learned volumes about photography and animals and more about waiting, but in four days, we have not seen one whale. This morning was gray when I got up and walked slowly to the edge of San Juan Island, where it dropped off into a cliff. Below, the waves were cutting away at the rock. Foott was already up, taking pictures of a wasps' nest he'd found the night before. A bald eagle glided above the water, and a dozen gulls fluttered near the cliff like moths. I was stretching my legs when I saw it. I thought I was dreaming.

A giant dorsal fin, like a dark sail, glided by in the fog. It was exactly as I'd pictured it, but much blacker and slower, cutting through the water like one tooth of the world's largest table saw. Our wait was over.

I hurried back to camp. Foott and I grabbed armloads of gear and in minutes were running down the rocky trail to the cove where Foott's boat was anchored. For days, while waiting in Jeff's van above the narrow strait through which killer whales are said to pass frequently, we had done fire drills in our minds rehearsing for that moment.

By the time we were out of the cove and up to full speed, Jeff figured we were half an hour behind the whales. The fourteen-foot *Boston Whaler* climbed the front of each swell and slapped down the back. Foott rode the boat as if it were a wild animal, his hair waving behind him, his eyes focused like lasers just beyond the bow, his legs absorbing each wave. I was trying to balance in the back, desperate to find the whales.

"There they are. They've stopped," he said, grinning at our good luck. Then he veered the boat right. I looked as hard as I could but saw nothing until a small, spouting geyser exploded in the distance. Foott turned the engine down and moved the boat carefully into position.

Then the wind died down, the water became calm, and we were waiting again. Watching Jeff reminded me of something that Spanish philosopher and writer José Ortega y Gasset said about a hunter knowing only that he does not know what will happen next. Jeff loaded film into his four cameras (two for "stills" and two for "cine") and wiped water droplets from his lenses, all without taking his eyes off the water, expecting anything. Expecting everything.

I try to relax, but I am too excited. Between my own breaths, my heart rattles inside my life preserver.

I have lost all sense of time and I am not sure if minutes or hours have passed when I see whales swimming just below the surface, an occasional tail flicking black, then white. Then we are surrounded by whales. They are longer than the boat, bigger than my imagination. I know that, technically, these animals are dolphins. But they are huge, and they scare me. A tall dorsal fin breaks the surface, tilts forward, and disappears. I want to touch it.

"Notch Fin," Foott says, referring to the obvious nick in the animal's fin. "He was here last year. It's been a good year—look at all the females with young."

They all look the same to me, a moving tangle of black bodies.

Ten yards away, a male breaches—comes almost completely out of the water—and splashes down on his side. With their white chin markings, these animals always seem to be smiling. Young ones spy-hop—poke their heads vertically out of the water to look around—disappearing when I make eye contact. One nudges the bottom of the boat, squeals, and makes clicking sounds like two pieces of thin, hard wood tapped together. Tails fan the air and the ocean boils as the whales play around the boat.

"What is going on?" I ask. The sea turns black, then white, then black again as these playful sea mammals roll over and over next to me. Strange sounds come at us from all directions.

"Don't know," Foott says, a huge movie camera at his eye. "Last year, I had the feeling they were reacting to my engine, as if they recognized it. Who knows?"

Before, while waiting in the van, I had read about sea mammals. Unlike humpback and blue whales, which are baleen, or filter-feeding, whales, killer whales *(Orcinus orca)* belong to the suborder Odontoceta, or toothed whales. They are members of the dolphin family, or Delphinidae. They might live to be eighty-five years old in the wild (forty or fifty in captivity), and a large male might grow to be thirty feet long and have a six-foot-high dorsal fin. They live in extended families called pods consisting of a few individuals to as many as forty. The pods appear to remain intact forever.

It turns out that whales and dolphins use two different voices, one to communicate and one to navigate and locate submerged objects. Their navigational voice functions like radar. They send clicks or rings that pass through the ocean until they meet an object of a different density from water. The sound waves bounce back, and the whale feels them in its giant jaw. The echoes are analyzed in the whale's brain, which processes information not only about the object's location but also about its shape, how fast it is moving, its texture and density, and its *internal structure*. In theory, a whale receiving an echo from a human swimmer knows not only the person's size and speed but also how he or she is feeling. One book says that these animals are constantly aware of one another's internal workings, health, and well-being and possibly of one another's emotional health as well. Whales, it seems, are living, breathing CAT scan machines.

What would it be like to live in an extended family in which individuals always know one another's emotions, feelings, and physical health, a family without secrets?

As quickly as it began, the action stops. Foott relaxes, reloads his cameras, and eats an Oreo. I am overcome by a feeling like love, but not exactly, and I feel a deep void now that they are gone. Jeff sees my disappointment and smiles.

"They'll be back."

I put my hand in the water and try to feel whale voices prodding me. I wonder if the whales are learning more about me than I know about myself. Foott and I scan all directions and wait. We are good at waiting. Waiting, though foreign to me in my regular life, is part of being a hunter. In business, waiting is not productive. Every moment must be full; there's not a second to waste. It's acceptable to write endless memos and make countless calls but never to be caught staring out the window. Waiting in the boat for whales represented a new, active form of the verb—not passive, as in waiting for someone who is late for an appointment or waiting for the clock to move or darkness to dissolve into light after a sleepless night.

Out here at sea, waiting has purpose. Time disappears completely. The entire world is right here—the sea, the sky, the island. Colors deepen. The rocks are alive; they just move more slowly than everything else. Everything is a sign or signal or symbol. I feel connected to those whales, as much when they are down deep, feeding, as when they are breathing in front of me. The absence of sound has its own sound.

During those fourteen-hour days in the van, I learned to wait without being restless. Foott and I traded off, one of us sleeping or reading while the other watched. Most of the time, we listened to music and talked while we waited.

Sometimes my mind got away from me and I worried about work. I thought about the meeting I'd just been to and how absurd that part of my life seemed once I got away from it. I

thought about the demonstration of water-saving toilets I'd witnessed in Seattle. It had taken place in a hotel conference room
with velvet walls and plush purple carpet. In the middle of the
room, a toilet sat on top of a large box. A long glass pipe
stretched from the box, angling down into a tub sixty feet away
at the other end of the room. No one laughed or even snickered
at the absurdity of the scene. This was important. A man in a
white lab coat put eight plastic balls into the toilet and flushed
it. Standing in lines on either side, grown men watched intently
as those balls floated through the pipe. The idea was to show
that this wondrous toilet could flush all eight balls—perfectly
designed to mimic human shit—out of the bowl, down the
entire length of the pipe, and into the tub, and accomplish the
entire feat using only one and one-half gallons of water. As we
watched the flushed balls move down the pipe, a luncheon buf-
fet was wheeled into the other end of the room.

I learned a lot from Jeff while we waited.

He taught me about ice and about how life is possible
because ice floats. Water is heaviest at 4 degrees centigrade, not
zero, its freezing point. Every other liquid gets heavier as it gets
colder. If water were heaviest at its freezing point, lakes and
oceans would freeze from the bottom up, killing everything.
Instead, mysteriously, water freezes from the top down; ice
floats on the surface, providing insulation to protect the earth's
complex aquatic systems. When Jeff learned about ice in high
school physics class, his entire perception of the universe
changed. He realized for the first time that life has a secret,
miraculous order, and the more he learned and watched, the
more sense he could make of the world.

Jeff talked about his sense that more is going on in the lives of wild animals than we know. When we watch them, he believes, we see only the outer manifestations of inner workings so intricate, archaic, and delicate that even imagining them is impossible. Complete understanding is out of the question.

I wondered about our own inner workings. What intricate forces lie deep and delicate inside us, and how many of them do we understand, let alone use in our lives? Not many. What have we lost by spending our brains on technology that eliminates the need for us to kill our own food, heal ourselves, predict the weather, and find our own way? And what price are we paying for not controlling our population because we have been lured into believing that we are the ultimate species and above the laws of nature and evolution?

Have we lost the power to save ourselves?

I spot a fin fifty yards away, and then a spout. Then four smaller fins and more spouting. Jeff fires up the engine and moves the boat closer. Then, in what appears to be a single, choreographed bow, the whales disappear.

We are in perfect position. Jeff has just shut off the engine when we hear a massive breath off the bow. My hair stands on end as the entire pod rises mysteriously, like the tide. I am sitting on the port gunwale when a huge body turns the sea next to me black. The male's dorsal fin passes within inches of my face.

I somehow expect that anything living in the sea must be fishlike, but leaning forward, I see millions of tiny hairs covering the whale's skin. I reach out and we touch, mammal to mammal. As his body moves under my fingers, I recognize something—brotherhood? An ancient relationship?

Then, without warning, the whale exhales and the air

explodes in a magical storm all around me. I sniff the watery cloud, then take a deep breath and feel it mixing inside my lungs. How familiar his breath smells, like air from a deep, old place, maybe a cave where I lived in another life. In an instant, he is gone.

As the pod surfaces for the third time, ten yards away, Jeff maneuvers the boat into position with one hand while holding a Nikon with the other. I watch a female exhale before completely breaking the surface. The surface tension fogs the interface of air and water, enclosing her in a glassy shell. Her six-foot-long baby rolls on his side, never out of touch. I am not aware of the exact moment when the "killer" part of the name loses its meaning, but I no longer feel any fear. The pod inhales and then sinks together, before me one second and gone the next, effortlessly.

Foott loads his cameras. He has shot 100 frames with his Nikon cameras and twenty-five feet of movie film; I haven't even noticed the whirring of the motor drives. Although Foott can't remember a time in his life when wild nature didn't fascinate him, he can pinpoint the exact day in 1950 when, after stalking a robin while sliding through the grass on his belly, he snapped his first picture. He was seven years old.

As early as junior high, he knew he could learn more outside the classroom than in it. He went to college only when he realized that he couldn't teach himself everything there was to learn about nature. He majored in biology and spent years studying and filming a family of sea otters before acknowledging that an academic career might mean studying one animal for the rest of his life, a commitment he wasn't prepared to make. Instead, he wanted to learn about as many different animals as possible. Foott found his passion in photography and had the courage to pick a fascinating, risky path over more comfortable and secure options.

In the silence while we waited again, I thought about breathing. Unlike humans, whales have separate passages for food and air; otherwise, they wouldn't be able to feed underwater. A whale breathes through the blowhole on top of its head, a slit surrounded by thick lips of elastic tissue. This slit is opened deliberately, and then only to breathe. What must it be like for a whale to stop whatever it's doing every five minutes and rise to the surface to breathe? What does it mean to breathe together as a family?

Buddhists believe that breathing is the prayer of the quiet, that consciousness expands when all concentration is directed toward breathing. By rejecting thought and reason, one can enter deeper areas of consciousness where intuition rises to the surface and with it a sense of well-being and integration. And I've read that couples sitting back to back, breathing together, without touching, can reach orgasm. Modern psychologists prescribe the breathing techniques used in transcendental meditation and the Zen practice of zazen for patients with emotional disorders, knowing that positive physical effects can be measured in the brain and body. Half an hour each day spent concentrating on air passing through our noses in an ancient rhythm can change our lives.

What if we were aware of *every* breath we took, like whales? What are we missing? What is sweeter than a fresh, entering breath, our bellies rising to contain it, the outer world's life-giving molecules mixing with our bodies? What emotional heights have been reached by animals who are reborn every time they break the ocean's surface to breathe? What does it mean to an individual body to have ancestors who have been breathing consciously, communally, for millions of years? Is the human imagination supple enough even to consider these questions?

The whales have surfaced again, a hundred yards south. They seem to have tired of feeding and lounge on the surface. One male's large dorsal fin quivers and leans and gradually tilts until ocean water enters his breathing hole, waking him up. The young ones seem curious about our boat. We float in close, and they bounce their snouts off the sides. Their nervous mothers herd them away until we turn off the motor.

My eye catches the eye of a male. His eye is large, like a glass net float, and reflects the clouds and sky in its smoky surface. A killer whale's eye is set in front of a white patch the size of a football that from a distance might be mistaken for the eye. Our eyes are not so different, the whale's and mine. But what about our minds? Scientists say that the whale's brain is 45 million years old; ours, only 2 million. How long before our species evolves enough to reach the humility and peace I feel exists among these whales?

Babies, full of energy, play tag between their lounging parents. One young male nudges his mother, trying to wake her, his pink penis erect and playful. She pushes him away with her tail.

They rub against one another. They purr and sigh. Seldom is one whale not in contact with one or two others. I dream about stripping off my clothes and slipping into the water while they nap, rubbing up against them. I imagine telling Foott that if something happens, if the whales mistake me for a seal and bite into me, or crush me by accident with their mass, to tell Terry that I always loved her and I didn't mind dying this way.

Even death seems a reasonable price. Some power pulls on me. I want to hold on to a dorsal fin and be pulled through the ocean, to be part of something that from my place on the deck of the *Boston Whaler* I can barely imagine. One hour is all I want. One hour with my body in constant contact with my fellow mammals, when each of my breaths is part of a family ritual. But I know that this underwater breathless world is not mine. I don't belong.

Flying home the next morning, I closed my eyes. Sleek black bodies rose around me; their breath was there in my lungs. I could feel it. What else had the whales and I been sharing? I had an errant thought: Baptism. My church puts eight-year-old children under the water after a sacred prayer. To wash away our sins? Or to remind us of whales?

I decided to make a list of commitments I would make to all animals:

No more hierarchy.
Speak quietly and don't move quickly in their presence.
Protect their habitats.
Study their behavior.
Open myself to a fuller extent of their knowledge.
Ritualize their lives.
Honor their deaths.

Back at my office, I found the following items on my desk: Five thick job files with notes stuck to them, two sets of approved submittals, three bids, four trade journals, a valve part I recognized, two catalogs I didn't, a bank statement, my day

planner opened to the next day with four appointments scheduled, miscellaneous personal letters, and an entire pad of telephone message notes.

Sighing, I got up and closed the door. Then I sat back down,
pulled out my notebook, and wrote:

> I've read that killer whales may be the most intelli-
> gent animals, second only to man. That may be true
> as long as man is making up the test. What if the
> whales made up the test? After watching them play
> and eat and touch and care about each other, I won-
> der if we humans possess the kind of intelligence to
> even measure theirs. The pressure inside me from
> pure feeling and emotion is taking up all available
> space.

Lois buzzed me on the intercom.

"It's Bart. He's been calling all week."

I picked up the telephone. Bart works for a large wholesaler.
"Hello."

"Brooke, it's Bart. How was your trip?"

"Incredible."

"You learned a lot?"

"So much, it may take years to sort it all out."

"How's the new generation?"

"Great. It was a good year—lots of young playing together.
They were constantly squealing and nudging the bottom of our
boat."

Silence.

"Bart, are you there?"

I suddenly realized that Bart and I were in different worlds.

I was talking about Puget Sound and whales; Bart was talking about the latest toilet technology.

"Brooke, this is a very confusing conversation."

I explained it all to him, and he pretended to be interested. He hadn't called to talk about whales. He'd called to talk about a problem with a water heater, one of twelve I'd sold him that had been installed in a new office building.

"The water is only lukewarm, and the tenants are pissed. Can you go look at it?" I tried to put him off for a few days, but the contractor was holding back money until Bart solved the problem. I made a note in my planner, told him I would check out the heater tomorrow, and hung up. Then I told Lois not to give me any more calls. I figured that all the paraphernalia in front of me was equally unimportant, so I put it all on the floor for later.

Then I called Terry, but the line was busy. I returned a call from my mother and compressed my trip into a breathless flurry of images about whales and water and Foott taking pictures. My life always fascinated my mother; she wanted to know every detail. When I finished, she said, "We've got to find a way for you to have work like that."

I called Terry again. Still busy. I got up, turned off the light, and left. I had to get home to tell her. My new world was too big and my office too small to contain it. It would be a while before I could care about lukewarm water.

Nine

I F JEFF FOOTT HAS THE PERFECT JOB, Sally Cole's is a close second. She has melded her love of art and her passion for exploration into a career as a rock art archaeologist. Under contracts with the Bureau of Land Management or the National Park Service, she reproduces the images chipped and painted on sandstone walls by ancient artists and records pertinent information within a strict set of guidelines. Her work is filed and made available to other archaeologists or anthropologists, who look at her reproductions when they want to compare the works of different cultures or even styles of individual artists, or use it in any other way that might make further sense of the rock art.

Rock art fascinated me the first time I saw the thousands of petroglyphs chipped into the sandstone's dark patina-like surface at Newspaper Rock, on the road to the Needles District in Canyonlands National Park. I wondered whether rock art is a language one culture uses to speak to another, even across long gaps of time. To understand it better, I once spent a week of my vacation taking a workshop taught by Sally. Ten of us met at Anasazi State Park in Boulder, Utah.

We talked, getting to know one another and wondering what

it would be like to spend a week together. Sally went over a list to make sure we had what we needed and then laid out our schedule. The next morning, we would drive for half an hour; then we would pick up our forty-pound packs, carry them all day to a secret rock art site, and document what we found there. She explained that documentation involves mapping the area, drawing the figures, and labeling them with dimensions and colors. This was important information. It would help the Bureau of Land Management better understand the people who once lived in the Gulch. Sally was working at her job, but I was on vacation.

It was just past dark when we threw our sleeping bags down on the grass next to the museum. About midnight, the gentle, scented breeze changed to huge gusts, scattering dirt and cottonwood branches. Then the rain came and we moved indoors, trading a wet night on soft grass for a roof and a hard floor. Before settling in, I walked around and looked at the exhibits of jewelry, pottery, and even the bones of the Anasazi people who had lived on the mound behind the building eight hundred years before. I rolled out my pad and sleeping bag beneath an exhibit of a recently excavated burial (it has since been removed, out of respect). A young woman adorned in turquoise had been buried surrounded by pottery, beads, and other items to help her make a smooth transition to the next world. Her importance to those who buried her was obvious.

Well before dawn, I was wide awake. The room was hot and I was sticky inside my sleeping bag, so I got up and went outside. The rain had stopped, but what it had done to the desert smelled so good. My mind glided between the excitement of what we might find in the canyon and the dread of what I'd left undone back at my job in Salt Lake City.

I waited until half past eight to call my office and retrieve my messages. Lois answered. Lois had started working for the company before I was born; she loved to tell customers about changing my diapers when I was a baby. Once she came into my office and said she had a problem. "I've been hearing about 'sexual harassment,'" she said, "and I'm wondering when it's going to start around here."

"Rex Williams & Sons," she answered, the same as always.

When I called the office from out of town, I had a bad habit of screaming into the phone as if I had to compensate for the distance. It always made her laugh.

"LOIS, I'M IN BOULDER, UTAH. CAN YOU HEAR ME?"

She laughed. I knew she had a pad of pink "While you were out" notes next to her phone, and by this time in the morning she'd have picked up the mail and would be on her second cup of coffee. We exchanged pleasantries but kept them short. She was from that old school of thought that long-distance calls were expensive, so we were always very efficient. "Any messages?" I asked.

"That sensor you had sent down to BYU (the one that automatically turns the faucet on when you put your hands under it)—well, they shipped one for a urinal, so the faucet won't turn on until they leave." She laughed. "One student thought he was on *Candid Camera*. I've got the right one coming. Those hundred faucets at the new Holy Cross Hospital: they're fine except they're missing the aerators. Your dad says he'll hire your little brother to install them when they get here. Bradley is shipping them by air freight. Down at Camp Williams, the column showers don't have check valves, and over the weekend hot water from the boiler forced its way through the shower and into the cold-water line. Now they get steaming water in the toilets in the next room. Sounds nice to me. The factory is working on it. And your mother called. She says, 'Have a good time,' and 'Oh, be careful.'"

"Sounds like you've got it all under control," I said. "Thanks for everything."

"Call next time you get a chance," she said. "Now, let me put your father on."

"Brooke, you're in Boulder. Great. Have a good time. We'll hold down the fort. Love you," my father said. He meant it.

After packing up and driving, we walked for five hours, crossing the creek at least twenty times. We'd just rounded a bend and pushed through willows higher than our heads when Sally stopped in her tracks next to an old, bent cottonwood tree, dropped her pack, and disappeared behind a dune. We followed her tracks and found her surrounded by a curving rock wall the size of a theater screen. Colored figures completely covered the wall.

We spent the first two days mapping the site, using compasses, protractors, and long tape measures. Then we began duplicating all the drawings. Someday, by looking at our drawings and comparing them with others, archaeologists might be able to make some sense of this art. So little is known about it. For now, rock art cajoles and confuses and makes hikers dream things they can't understand. I had been assigned my own section of this rock art panel, and I'd been looking at it for twenty hours. This was not work in the way I knew work.

The first drawings I copied were familiar: a buck deer with antlers like tree branches, a desert bighorn with curling horns. I felt a very old and foreign hand alongside mine as I sketched.

Then I was working on images I didn't understand. They were large figures, forty centimeters tall, with broad shoulders, heads with horns, and no visible means of connecting with the ground. They were black—not just black but 7.5R 2.5/0 on the hue circle of the Munsell color system. And dusky red (10R 3/4) and reddish yellow. Sally stopped to look over my shoulder. "The style," she said. "You can't get it out of your skin."

She said the figures I was working on were Barrier Canyon style with some Chihuahuan polychrome abstract, technical classifications that hint at when and by whom the paintings were made. The paint contains hematite, and over time the figures had become part of the rock. Sally sat quietly. I could feel her fire. Her fire became music, and the figures almost danced.

I moved to get a different angle and saw a drawing of an insect with a long neck, a large, bottle-like abdomen, and antennae the full length of its body. I wasn't sure what it was, but at the moment I didn't care. I wanted to know what inspired these drawings. The evening before, as the insects were tuning up, Sally had wandered away from the fire just as I'd grabbed an armload of bottles and our pump to go for water. I had followed. Rock art is only one reason why Sally comes back to these canyons over and over again. She returns, she says, to feel more connected to those who lived here a thousand years ago. I walked fast to catch up. There was still daylight, and I could see her long hair bouncing from side to side off her back. Sally believes that hair is power, and she rarely cuts hers.

"It's really a misnomer, the term *rock art*," she'd said as I caught up, but as if she would have been saying it anyway, out loud to no one.

"*Rock* or *art*?" I asked. Dusk purpled our skin.

"Art," she said. "I read somewhere that Indian people have

no word for art in their native language because it is basic to everything in their lives."

"Who painted on the walls?" I asked her in a loud whisper. Earlier in the week, we had discussed the differences between the Anasazi people, who farmed and built stone villages such as Chaco, Keet Seel, and Mesa Verde, and the Desert Archaic people, the older hunter-gatherers, who painted the figures on our wall. But I wanted something more specific, and Sally knew it.

"Probably a shaman," she said. (I'd become used to words like *probably* in our conversations. Sally never wanted to sound too sure about something one generation can never really know about another.) She told me about shamanism and about primitive religions and spirits that can be controlled for healing and the sorting out of good and evil. She told me that shamanism involves leadership, mystery, and magic. "It's an amazing concept," she said. "The heavy responsibility of receiving visions and giving people hope. It's not a highly revered position."

I asked her why one would want to do it.

She said, "They have no choice. They're picked in another life," as if that explained it.

In his book *The Old Ways,* Gary Snyder wrote that a shaman speaks "for the wild animals, the spirits of the plants, the spirit of the mountains, of watersheds. . . . They sing through him."

We walked past a dune that was covered with yellow composites, flowers that seemed to glow in the lowering light. I turned and walked up a small side canyon to the pool that had become our water supply. The same wind that had moved enough sand to cover my footprints from the day before had exposed a stone point, two thousand years old. The wind had blown time into a circle. Later, I went to sleep wondering what it is in our lives for which we have no word.

Trying to imagine a shamanic relationship with the supernatural sent a charge through me. A shaman, sitting here in this sand a thousand years ago—inspired by something he or she had seen somewhere in a world much bigger than and different from mine—had painted an image on the wall.

I wanted to travel back through the art, through the paint dabbed on the rock to the fingers holding the wet stick, to the mind, neuron to neuron, in a million steps through the artist's eyes to the source. What was this really, this large, horned figure coming at me through the wall? The artist's brain and mine were the same; so was this landscape. Had I been reprogrammed? Or was something missing from my modern world, something so ancient that I would never understand this painting? Was I separated from the art in the same way I can never know the pain of a hook in a fish's mouth or what sex feels like to a woman?

We were four days into the trip, and something was happening to me. Part of my transformation had to do with camping out and living beneath a cliff, just as my human predecessors had lived here two thousand years ago. But part had to do with a force coming from a different part of my brain. I'd found a new channel, one having nothing to do with profits or valves. This new force worked smoothly, seductively, anchoring my mind, not letting it wander. I was riveted to these rocks. The feeling was almost sexual.

I returned from the trip to descend into a low, dark place. I knew too well from my week in the wilderness that all I really need I can carry on my back and that when given the opportunity, my body functions extraordinarily well: smooth joints, effortless movement, senses sharp as razors. I knew, too, the difference between watching a fingernail moon move across the full sky and watching television. I realized that paying pure, uninterrupted attention stimulates me. But my life seemed burdened with the details—the sick cat, the overflowed holding tank that filled the basement with sewage. Even the shower partitions I forgot to order and the pissed-off people Lois had to deal with, the phone call I didn't have time to make that meant losing an important contract because I didn't meet the price. And so I fell into a depression brought about by knowing that most of our stresses have recently been added to our lives. At the same time, I realized that stress need not be part of my life, and yet it was. In my depression, I failed to consider the differences in my halflives.

Ten

REGARDLESS OF WHY I DROP INTO A DARK FUNK on returning from a wild adventure, running is a quick cure. Sometimes, it is all I can do to drive myself to a trailhead where even the seatbelt buckle seems too complicated to open. Other times, my memory of how good running makes me feel acts like a drug and I find myself moving along a trail, having never actually decided to do it, and not remembering how I got there.

I don't run every day, but when I do run, running is the best part of my day. It should be. It is a wild act—active, innate, natural, but never tame, never domesticated. I began running at night just to stay in shape. I measured out a three-mile route on the road past the first small cottage where Terry and I lived. Then I started taking my running shoes and shorts to work, and instead of lunching with customers, I would drive up the hill from my office to my parents' house and change there. Then I'd run on the dirt roads and trails through the foothills I had explored as a kid. My mother would feed me lunch, and we would talk. I found that running was a way to compress more wild space into less time. What had once been all-day hikes were now lunch-hour runs.

The foothills separating Salt Lake City from the Wasatch

Range are not spectacular in the way that the mountains whose pictures appear in calendars are, but from their tops, I always get dizzy watching the beauty of the late-day colors spread across Great Salt Lake. I've learned a lot, running in those hills. Important things have occurred to me there.

When life gets too busy, with everything baled and stored like hay, running spreads it out where I can look at it. No matter how stressed I am, ten minutes into a long run, when my muscles are warm and loose and my joints are working smoothly, something mysterious takes over. My heart's effort in pushing my body along the trail forces blood and chemicals into every dark capillary of my brain, washing dormant cells alive. I am reminded of the way bodies are intended to feel. The sensation makes me think of migrating monarch butterflies, who "remember" the way even though they have never been there, as if there must be a cellular memory. Running is the connection, the trigger, like touching wires. Cells light up, heat up, begin to hum with energy.

One afternoon, I turned on the radio and heard two men talking with each other while they ran together. As I listened, I learned that they were trying to catch pronghorn antelope in the desert near Rock Springs, Wyoming. The two runners, Scott Carrier and his brother, David, were testing the idea that primitive hunters could actually chase an animal until it was tired enough to catch and kill. David, an anthropologist, has written extensively on the subject of human running and breathing and believes that among mammals, humans are some of the best distance runners. In his paper "The Energetic Paradox of Human Running and Hominid Evolution," Carrier cited research on the physiology of modern humans and evidence suggested by the fossil record to make the case that even before early hominids developed hunting weapons, they may have been "endurance predators equipped with biological weapons."

The Carriers' plan was to identify one individual pronghorn and chase it in a circle. They would separate and David would run for a while, chasing the animal toward Scott, who would then chase it back to David. The idea was to keep the animal running sporadically in a circle until it was exhausted. But the runners got tired before the pronghorn did, probably because they had trouble making sure they were always chasing the same animal. Next time, they plan to try keeping the tiring pronghorn away from its friends to be certain they aren't always chasing a fresh one. Or maybe they will shoot it with a paintball gun so they can be sure they are always chasing the same animal. And they'll get more of their friends to help. David knows the method works. The !Kung bushmen in Africa hunt duikers, steenboks, wildebeest, and zebras by running them down. Tarahumara Indians chase deer through the mountains of northern Mexico, and Paiute and Navajo hunters have taken pronghorn antelope this way.

Our "biological weapons" are simple. In our not-too-distant evolutionary past, we lost our hair and developed a sophisticated system of sweat glands, which enable us to raise our metabolic rate for sustained periods. To appreciate the physiological advantage we have, look at the cheetah, which can run much faster than a human but only for short distances. It can run 100 kilometers per hour for up to 1 kilometer, which is as far as it needs to run at that speed to catch most of its prey. Covered with hair, the cheetah can dissipate heat only from its mouth and tongue, so after 1 kilometer it needs to lie down and pant. It stops not because it is tired but because its body temperature is too high.

Every summer, humans run in places and at speeds that would mean death to any other animal. In California, runners race across Death Valley to the top of Mount Whitney in less than thirty hours in the Badwater Race. In Utah, hundreds of runners enter a drawing for the opportunity to run for twenty-four hours up and down a section of the Rocky Mountains in the Wasatch Front 100 Mile Endurance Run, and on July 24, thousands run the route their ancestors took into the Great Salt Lake Valley in the Pioneer Day marathon.

Such physical exertion is possible only because humans sweat instead of pant. Our wet skin provides much more surface area for evaporative cooling, which is further enhanced by the air being pulled across our moving bodies. Perhaps our early brothers learned they were more successful hunting rabbits when they chased them during the hot, middle of the day rather than in the early morning. Humans have the advantage of running on two legs, not four. When a four-legged animal runs, its chest muscles and bones absorb the shock of its front legs hitting the ground. This motion compresses the space inside the chest so that the animal must breathe mid-stride, once each step cycle. In contrast, humans can breathe as often as needed, depending on speed and terrain. A quadruped has one gait, one efficient speed. We have many; for us, running is like riding a bike with ten gears instead of one. By forcing prey to run faster than it prefers to run or by making it continually slow down and speed up, we can theoretically wear it down and kill it with the most primitive weapons.

Humans run well for other reasons. Our adrenal and thyroid glands can increase the output of hormones critical for running.

And our omnivorous diet allows us to store more glycogen, fuel for the long chase.

Running, then, is a natural and wild act.

After a winter of grays and browns, the foothills are a colorful pallet, tinted green from all the new grasses, mixed with pink and white from spring beauties, and yellow from glacier lilies growing in the shade of oaks. I leave the office to run to the top of Mount Van Cott to watch the sun set. I drive as high above the city as the paved roads go and park in the upper University Hospital parking lot. By pulling in close to another car and opening both doors on the passenger side, I can create a small dressing room. I've learned to strip quickly but carefully enough not to indecently expose myself. I change, stow my keys in their secret place, and take off without stretching. I never stretch. I should, but I don't. The trail is steep for the first hundred yards, and I move slowly to loosen up, almost walking. I glance back, west. Great Salt Lake, a water body the size of Delaware and Rhode Island combined, forms a silvery purple line against the horizon. I smell the brine and silt being blown up by the wind twenty miles away. After a fast quarter mile, I swerve right, up a spur aimed at the summit. My body down-shifts; my stride shortens. My breaths change from one every three steps to one step, one breath, the rhythm of it becoming a force of its own.

The spur trail is divided into fourths: a steep section that I need to walk up; a twisting, rocky roller coaster; another vertical walk; and then a gradual cutback to the summit. Midway up the third section, I smell death.

Then I see the antler, a two-point like a large wishbone. I

have found many deer parts in these hills—entire skulls with teeth; thin, flat scapulas that are almost translucent. On occasion, I have come face to face with the living animal stirred there on the trail, both of us stunned, confused about who is predator and who is prey. I have seen red foxes and Cooper's hawks. Once, I saw a mountain lion, but from such a distance that I could not be sure with my eyes—the long, low form, half of it tail, that's all I saw. But I *knew* it was a mountain lion. Often, the indescribable becomes irrefutable.

There are always lots of birds: ravens, magpies, black-capped chickadees, lazuli buntings with blue backs as shocking as the red heads of western tanagers. One fall day, I experienced what I thought was an earthquake when a huge covey of chukars got up all at once; they made the entire hillside move. I saw a goshawk with a mouthful of feathers. There are red-tailed hawks, which I always hear before I see—lots of them.

I stoop down to reach for the antler, sweat dripping off my nose, and hear something inside me say, *Don't run with the antler. You could fall on it, stab yourself in the chest, in the lung, maybe, and die there alone, blood foaming out of your mouth.* I stand there. I wait for the voice again to see whether it is real. *Don't run with the antler.* I realize that the voice comes to me not in words but in pure feelings; my mind converts the amorphous feelings into words. I think about the antler's sharp points, the hardness of bone. The danger running with that antler might add to my life. God forbid I should fall (I have fallen many times), and yes, the antler could puncture my lung or my heart. Blood would foam, wouldn't it, mixing with the air in the lungs? Dying alone is not my fear. My fear is always for Terry, who never knows where I will run on any particular day because I never know until I get there. I think about her at home, where she is waiting, and I don't come and the horror of her not knowing where ever to begin looking.

I pick up the antler, realizing that the feeling is not telling me what to do but sending me a warning:

Don't run with the antler, and *Run carefully with the antler.* Knowing the difference between these two statements may be what I am most proud of in my life. The risk, the danger—it lets me be born over and over and over again. It keeps me centered, like love. Antler in hand, I sprint up the last section of the trail, all my senses on high, lighting the way.

Eleven

N *ATURAL:* PRODUCED BY NATURE, not artificial, innate. Growing without human care. Untouched by civilization or society. *Wild:* being in a state of nature, not inhabited, not tame or domesticated. Passionately eager or marked by turbulent agitation.

The two words are closely related, but my sense is that the word *wild* adds action to what is natural. A wild river is natural, but a natural river is not necessarily wild. Certainly the part of my life that is wild is easy to identify. But what about my natural life? Curious, I decided to record my daily routine to determine how much of my day is natural, innate, and not artificial.

At six o'clock in the morning, the cat jumps on our bed, waking me. Lying there, fading in and out of consciousness, I dream about a man I know drowning in a pool filled with garbage. Dreams are clearly a natural process, personal glimpses into our unconscious mind using symbols as the language. Mythologist and folklorist Joseph Campbell believes that we share symbols with every human who ever lived. The keeping of cats and other pets, though, is not exactly natural. According to Paul Shepard in his book *Nature and Madness,* pet keeping is a "civilized institution, an abyss of covert and unconscious uses of animals in the service of psychological needs, glossed over as play and companionship." He goes on to say that before civilization, animals belonged to their own "nation." In the village, they became possessions.

I get up and stumble into the bathroom to relieve myself, pushing the button on my new Crane 3-604 Economizer toilet complete with the Flushmate state-of-the-art system that will flush away any sign with just one and one-half gallons of water. Certainly the act of urination is natural—every organism generates and eliminates waste products. Yet toilets and plumbing and sewers, as lucrative as they are for Rex W. Williams & Sons, are not natural. Won't we be surprised to learn that the nutrient cycle we disrupt by treating sewage is more important than we once thought?

I get into the shower, just as I do every morning. But why? I don't think it's necessary to keep as clean as I do. Taking too many showers plays havoc with skin and hair, wastes water, and consumes energy. Only a hundred years ago, my pioneer ancestors were content with a Saturday night bath. And certainly Arctic explorers have gone months without bathing, as have climbers on long expeditions to high mountains where the only water comes from melted snow. The point is that we can get only so dirty, and we probably don't need all the sweet-smelling soap and deodorizers to help mask our natural scent. How is it that we have been conditioned to dislike our natural, human body odors?

I dry myself, dress in synthetic fibers, and head for the kitchen. Hunger is natural; what is unnatural are the choices facing me. Eggs and bacon with cholesterol? Doughnuts for the sugar buzz? Toast with jam? Yogurt? Or bran flakes for fiber? And then, which brand of bran flakes? There are dozens. All day long, I am faced with too much food and too many choices about what to eat.

As I drive to work, I remember a story about an Australian Aborigine who, riding in a car, couldn't sing fast enough to know the way because he had learned the song's map by walking. Modern transportation has compressed space into unknown quantities. I put 40,000 miles on my car every year. On the radio I hear news from all over the world. Fifteen thousand years ago, before civilization, 5 million people wandered the earth in bands of 30 to 50 individuals, the members of each band thinking they were all alone in the world.

At work, I begin talking on the telephone. Most calls come from customers who have questions about the products I sell. "How do I install the new flush valve?" "Where is my shipment?" "Can't you give me a lower price?" "Why won't any of our new wash fountains shut off?" I am put off by the calls until I remember that this is part of my job. I've read all the catalogs and have been to technical sessions, so I am the "expert," the one everyone wants to talk to.

I am one of a growing number of Americans who don't produce anything that can be held in the hand. Most of us are somewhere in the middle, getting paid to be one more link in the chain connecting producer to consumer, the two poles generating the force that now seems to keep the earth spinning. This is part of my struggle. I need to know that I make a difference; I need to know that what I do all day is good beyond meeting my own personal needs and those of my family.

My father brings me a note from one of our suppliers about the potential for selling 200 expensive faucets for a large hotel being planned at a new ski resort east of Provo. He knows that I've been involved in a movement to stop the Forest Service from approving the resort on the grounds that it will negatively affect a beautiful, pristine area. Do I restrain myself from taking the opportunity to make the company and myself a lot of money? Do I continue working to protect the natural forest? My father senses my ambivalence and trusts that I'll do what I think is right. Restraint must be unnatural or it wouldn't be so difficult to practice.

Before lunch, I attend a short meeting to discuss my retirement plan. I have done very little to ensure that Terry and I will be comfortable financially should we live longer than we can be productive. Our early ancestors knew that their children would care for them in their old age.

In the evening, I drive to my health club. I change my clothes and go downstairs to the machine room. I climb onto a stationary bicycle and program it for twelve minutes. I look around and laugh. Besides eight people pedaling stationary bikes, there are six people walking in place on treadmills and four climbing stairs that are moving in the opposite direction they are trying to go. We are all on moving machines but going absolutely nowhere. For many of us, exercise has become the process of hooking ourselves up to a machine that adds something that's missing from our lives. Health clubs are a pure reminder that our bodies are made for a different world from the one we live in.

I leave the bike and move into another room where people, mostly women, are waiting for the start of an aerobics class. A beautiful woman probably half my age sets her steps directly in front of me. She wears pink tights and a leotard with the sides cut up to her waist. Her long, blond hair is pinched back in a ponytail, and she smells terrific. Part of my attraction to her might have something to do with the fact that men's testosterone levels increase in the fall. Karen Wright wrote for *M Magazine* that if this "seems to run counter to the popular notion about a young man's fancy, bear in mind that our species evolved below the equator, where fall is spring." We begin by bending and stretching to a familiar song, the beat more a vibration I feel than a sound I hear. The woman in pink does not have one ounce of fat, at least that I can see, and I can see most of her.

I wonder about my attraction to that woman. Although the modern media would have us believe that only thinness is attractive, the chubby women depicted in Renaissance paintings defined beauty for that era and still do in some cultures today. When the percentage of body fat in modern female athletes gets too low, they stop menstruating and can't get pregnant. This is evolution's way of limiting the population when food is scarce. Shouldn't I be more attracted to a plump woman with a better chance of bearing a healthy child?

Later, at home, Terry is making dinner—chicken because it is lower in cholesterol and supposedly better for the heart than red meat. Everything we eat comes from the grocery store and is grown and harvested or manufactured by others.

After dinner, we clean up and talk and then sit down to read. Terry picks up something by some French deconstructionist feminist, and I find a review of *The Manufacture of Evil: Ethics, Evolution, and the Industrial System* by Lionel Tiger. One paragraph haunts me:

> Man is a complex primate, physiologically still geared to be a hunter and gatherer, now forced to live in the artificial world made by modern technology. He is ill-prepared for this. . . . This does not

mean that we cannot go against our nature in our belief and behavior. But there will be costs to such "unnatural" acts. The costs are mounting.

I have not walked on one natural surface all day, only on cement or tile or the spring-loaded carpet on the aerobics floor. What haunts me is how full of "unnatural acts" all our lives are. The costs *are* mounting.

When we tire of reading, Terry sits on me and puts her hand inside my shirt. My body responds naturally. After twenty years of marriage, we have our signals. So far, we have chosen not to have children. Yet there is nothing the slightest bit natural about members of a species deciding not to conceive and give birth. If everyone were as ambivalent about having children as we are, our species would become extinct. But as unnatural as it is, if we don't work to control our exploding population, it will most likely be the factor that destroys us.

Our blood picks up steam; our hearts pound. We move upstairs, fitting together in bed like the perfect puzzle. Lying there spooned together, I hold one of her breasts. When I am not moving, my hand ceases being a hand and her breast is no longer a breast. Neither is neither. Movement is required for definition. Dynamics define the world. We are meant to move.

Twelve

O NE'S NOT HALF OF TWO, it's two are halves of one." Terry had this line from an e. e. cummings poem engraved on the back of a rough piece of silver. A couple, holding hands, is soldered on the front. It is attached to a chain, and I used to wear it around my neck. She gave it to me when we were married because I didn't want to wear a ring; I told her that everyone would know I was married by the smile on my face. She rolled her eyes. Thinking back to the poem, although I wanted to believe it, I'm not sure I ever did. "Two are halves of one": becoming "one," "of one flesh," is something every young couple should aspire to—or so we've always been taught. But what does it mean?

Terry seems to have known her way in the world from an early age. Mimi, her grandmother, always said that Terry was an "old soul." Mimi had home movies showing Terry at age eight performing pagan rituals at Christmas. People who believe in reincarnation would say that Terry has "been around many times"—had many prior lives. I've been around only a few, which may explain why Terry has been so supportive during my struggle to learn life's lessons. She says it's reciprocal because I rescued her from the life she was expected to lead—

that of a perfect Mormon wife: the quiet, loving half of a patri-archal marriage, relief society president, soccer mom, etc. A few months after we married, Terry's mother and I were talking alone. She apologized for not having taught Terry the basics of homemaking. "I wanted her to know how to cook and keep house," she said, "and I tried; I honestly tried. But I realized that it was not in her makeup. Her mind was always somewhere else, and to push her might mean sacrificing our friendship, which I was not willing to do."

Later, her father thanked me for taking Terry off his hands. "She was driving me crazy. Mundane details don't mean any-thing to her," he said. "She never gets with the program. She would block the driveway with her car and then lose her keys. She's a dreamer."

Terry doesn't have halflives, a fact that I find to be simulta-neously the most frustrating and the most inspiring aspect of our marriage. This is evident in her ability to focus completely on whatever she is doing at the time. When she writes, she only writes—for days or weeks at a time and sometimes for a month. When she is teaching, she is only teaching. During a one-day workshop or spring quarter, teaching is all she thinks about. When she is with family, that's it. When she reads, she does not answer the telephone, change the sprinklers, or move clothes from the washer to the dryer. When she talks on the phone, it's for an hour. When she cooks, she uses all the pans. When we eat out, it takes all night. When we talk, we change. And when she is gone, she is far away.

"Becoming one" may work best if teamwork is the main goal. But what is lost, what pieces do we cut off ourselves in order to fit together?

One doesn't work for me. Two is better. We give each other support and remove obstacles when we can. Over the years, we have come to understand each other's needs. On a recent hike, we'd been out for half an hour when Terry found a perfect perch cut into a sandstone ledge with a stream running by and decided to sit there while I ran five miles, out to a scenic overlook and back. Becoming one would have meant the two of us walking out to the overlook, at a pace slower than mine and faster than hers, and would have meant frustration for both of us. We realized early in our marriage that our insisting on skiing together every week would be disastrous—Terry wandering off to follow a set of squirrel tracks while I waited, wishing I were skiing off the high ridge in the distance. We ski alone, each at our own pace. When we go backpacking together, Terry knows she will end up in a more beautiful and remote place than if she went alone. I know that with her, each step of the way will have new dimensions of light and color and intricate detail.

In our case, we are lucky to have parallel pasts (we grew up within five miles of each other, and our parents have friends in common but had never met) and are luckier still to share a worldview.

Three is best. The third thing is somehow longer than two, placed end to end. "One plus one equals three," Terry's grandmother Mimi always said. Maybe e. e. cummings was referring to the third thing when he said that two are halves of one. If so, he forgot to mention that it works only if those two remain intact. Otherwise, the individuals disappear in the process.

Although Terry and I don't have children, we take some solace in my father's comment that for years he and my mother "worried you weren't going to have children and then worried that you would" when they began to accept our seminomadic lifestyle. In many ways, I believe that Terry and I have given birth to each other.

At its worst, our marriage is lonely. At its best, Terry holds up a mirror for me while providing a safe place for me to deal with what I see. I do the same for her. In between, we read the *Sunday Times* at brunch, argue over a hawk (is it a rough-legged or a Swainson's?), go for long walks, take trips, and trade massages. I *know* I am more than I would be without her. I think she is too. Three is bigger than one or two. Three can be huge.

Thirteen

H ALFLIVES DON'T BOTHER MY FRIEND GLEN LATHROP, who
may know as much about the Colorado Plateau as anyone. During his fifty years, he has known enough people who
spend one part of their lives cultivating a passion and another
part selling out, transforming their passion into something mar-
ketable for money to live on. Great skiers end up teaching
beginners to snowplow. World-class climbers show overweight
rich people how to move on uneven surfaces and tie knots. Talented artists and writers create brochures to help companies
sell computers or feminine hygiene products. Curious scientists
work for 3M or for a government testing laboratory.

Selling out is not an option for Glen. He could make a decent
living working as a guide, exposing tourists to places they could
never dream of. But he doesn't. For starters, he doesn't like to
waste time talking. He also firmly believes that a key element of
a spectacular place is a dearth of people. Above all, he loves
unplotted exploration too much. He thrives on finding new
places he's not sure how to get to, not knowing whether he'll
need a rope or a wetsuit, an hour or a week. He earns money
managing a paving company south of Moab, a small town in the
heart of Utah's canyon country.

For Glen, four o'clock in the afternoon, with the office door slamming behind him, signals the end of one halflife and the beginning of the other. He spends the remaining daylight hours wandering sandstone rims or exploring deep, unknown canyons. At night, he studies maps and plans his next trip. He lives simply in a small house. He was married once and has an open and caring nature that women find attractive, but his blue truck with its odometer pushing 300,000 miles and an ammo can for a passenger seat frightens them away. Nearly all the money he makes he saves for traveling.

Every winter, when business slows down, Glen travels to far-away places. He has visited all the world's major mountains and deserts. He has been to China and Nepal, been mugged in Morocco, seen a valley of human skeletons in the Sahara. He has seen temples carved in sandstone in the Middle East and giraffe petroglyphs in Namibia.

Glen follows politics only so far as it affects the wild places he loves. Otherwise, the weather report is the only news he needs. When he is gone, people will tell stories about Glen. Some already do.

There are the stories of how he treats his cats like people, hanging cat pictures on his walls at cat's-eye level. Or the technique he's developed for cooking microwave meals from the supermarket over a small fire. Or how he sails on Lake Powell in the moonlight, hops freight trains, and closes dirt roads with a crowbar and chain, or about his garden, his carport, and all his weird watercraft. But some of Glen's own best stories are about how he finds women. Some stories are wild and scary and involve personal ads, European trains, and even a Chinese computer scientist. My favorite, however, is the standing deal he has with Tom-Tom, the local Volkswagen repairman. Every time a woman matching a fairly general description needs help with her Volkswagen, Tom-Tom calls Glen, who "just happens" to walk by, introduces himself, and offers to take the woman for a hike while her car is being worked on. If Glen likes her, he gets word to Tom-Tom, who suddenly finds that the car needs a part from Salt Lake City. Glen met Laura this way; they lasted five years. Glen could be a book.

Glen and I share weekends—since 1980, maybe 75 of them. (An average of 1 every two months for 200 months, minus 50 for winters when he's traveling, divided by 2, equals 75 trips.) We give ourselves problems to solve. We look at maps, read guidebooks, and talk to people about different places or routes. We have followed maps drawn on the backs of coasters in smoky bars and on napkins covered with the juice of chicken-fried steak. Treasure maps. Often, we forget the problem within the first mile of walking; other times, we don't. For example, Glen once read about a complex of Anasazi ruins in an old report from Harvard University's Peabody Museum. We knew it had been excavated in the 1940s and approximately where it was. Even though we've been to the area four times, we've never found it, but we don't really care because we've seen amazing views, found potsherds and arrowheads, and spent ten nights camping out, which is a major part of it.

One trip stands out.

I forget the nature of the problem to be solved or even if there was one. I remember the trip starting as they all do, on a Friday afternoon, when the business world eases into the weekend. I'd packed the night before and stashed my gear in my Jeep. It was October and dark when I pulled up to Ray's Tavern in Green River. Glen was already there, stretched out in the back booth watching the scene.

Ray's is the place where most trips to the area begin and
end. The walls are covered with photographs and a collection of
T-shirts from every imaginable river company. The river season
was over, but the place was packed with mountain bikers heading for Moab. Glen had been watching for me and got up before
I could sit down. He was wearing his "Pave the World" hat to
throw people off.

"Been here long?"

"Since eight. Twenty minutes too long. Bikers drive me
crazy. Can't anyone hike anymore?"

"Anyone you know?"

"You kidding? You're not hungry, are you?"

"Sort of."

"I've got a cooler. Let's get out of here."

His pack and cooler were hidden in the corner.

We loaded his gear and headed west for Robbers' Roost
country.

Aptly named, the area had been one of the three main hide-
outs for outlaws in the West during the nineteenth century. The
most famous band of outlaws, the Wild Bunch, was headed by
Robert Leroy Parker, also known as Butch Cassidy. No one can
figure out how a good Mormon boy who grew up on a farm in
southern Utah could go on to lead a group of outlaws on a spree
of bank and train robberies spanning twenty years and two continents.

At eleven o'clock, Glen had me slow down and turn off on a
dirt road.

"How much farther?"

"About an hour."

"You've been here before."

"Not exactly."

The headlights lulled us into thinking that that huge invisible world out in the dark was nonexistent and that only what was illuminated—the roadside Russian thistles, the million splattered insects on the windshield, the occasional golden-mantled ground squirrel crossing in front of us or the deer mouse or great horned owl—was all there was.

The road finally ended by turning back on itself in a tight circle. We threw out our sleeping bags, and I turned off the headlights. There was no moon, but even in the darkness I could feel the real size of the world, and it was huge. How easy it is to forget to believe in anything we can't see.

I wake up when the first light spills out of the east. We are camped on a point, surrounded on three sides by a landscape different from anything I'd imagined the night before—sandstone domes and parallel fins, as if the earth's surface had been raked by the claws of a monster bird. There are veined canyons glowing from the cottonwoods changing color in their bottoms.

We finish packing and eating just as the sun rises.

We make a quick check of the map, shoulder our packs, and drop off the edge into the shadowed part of a side canyon of Robbers' Roost, part of the proposed Dirty Devil Wilderness Area.

Many people believe that a line divides the modern, "regular" world from wilderness. Members of different political persuasions have made many maps, each with his or her own idea of where that line should be. For each of those maps, there are whole organizations of people who know the exact reasons why those lines are where they are.

Glen and I know that we will cross the line into wilderness

this morning, though we don't know the exact moment. It is not painted on the rock. If it matters, we will certainly notice. Maybe one of our breaths will be deeper than the one before it. We might feel a lightness in our step or turn toward a sound that isn't there. But nothing. For me, the line dividing civilization from wilderness has never been a political boundary. It is more philosophical—religious, even. Thousands of us have been forced to deal with the nitty-gritty of boundaries, rules, and requirements of wilderness but none of the breath and blood of wildness. As a society, do we despise the word *wild?* Have we tamed what of it we could, then crossed it out of our lives? Some of us think we have. The problem is that wildness gets in the way of how our leaders want this modern world to work. What they fail to realize is that although they may succeed in erasing wildness from our minds, they can't remove it from our bodies.

In Robbers' Roost canyon country, topographic maps and guidebooks are useful for telling us whether, say, we are in the right canyon. But when 1 inch equals 24,000, the maps aren't much help. Out there, amazing and horrible things can happen in the forty feet between contour lines. Sometimes a trail will appear on a map, but rarely in the right place. Route finding becomes a challenge and then a skill. Geologic maps are more important, but nothing measures up to experience. After years of hiking, Glen and I have learned, for example, that the long, purple Kayenta ramps sitting above the Windgate cliffs in Canyonlands National Park are similar to the Supai in the Grand Canyon. We've learned that the rocks are different in Zion Canyon and the Escalante canyons. We know which formations will allow us through and which won't and that exceptions will always appear if we look long enough.

We climb down through Navajo Sandstone, a light-colored

rock formed during the Jurassic period when windblown sand
was compressed by the weight of more sand or silt from the bottoms of ancient oceans. We move down about thirty feet, walking on solid rock tilted to the edge of traction. Then onto a
ledge, where we move horizontally above a wall too long and
steep to risk climbing down, and then into another vertical section. We move quickly. I feel my body constantly computing the
ratio of my center of gravity to the traction of my soles against
the rock, to tell me when to stop relying on friction and reach
for a handhold. We veer left horizontally, for no rational reason.
In an hour, we find only a dead end and are forced to backtrack.
We carry a rope but will use it only if we come to a vertical layer
that is too smooth and dangerous to down-climb without it and
impossible to climb around.

Near the canyon bottom, we come to that layer. We wander
along it in one direction for ten minutes, then in the other for
twenty before finding the lowest point, still some fifty feet above
our goal.

"Looks like this is it," I say to Glen. Below me, the rock is
rounded, curving in underneath me.

"Time to pull out the rope?" Using the rope is a problem. If
we pull it down after using it, in order to have it with us should
the same situation arise later, we will be forced to find a new
route back to the car. If we leave it in place to help us over this
obstacle on the way out, we won't have it with us if we need it
farther along.

"In a minute. There's a small ledge below me." I step onto it
and am amazed by what I see.

"Glen. Moqui steps."

Slightly rounded by erosion over a thousand years, these
holes were carved into the rock for use as stairs by people

migrating between canyon rim and bottom. I turn, face the rock, and lower my left leg until I find the first hole; then I lower my right leg and my left again, finding each hole exactly where it should be. There are eight steps. We feel a sense of pride in having found what must be the best route into the canyon, but pride soon gives way to the realization that it makes perfect sense. We have the same bodies and brains as the people who made the steps while moving through this country long ago. Why wouldn't we find the same route, especially if there were only one?

At the bottom of the Moqui steps, we follow a wide ledge into an alcove, which seems like a good place to camp. At the entrance, we find pictographs of bighorn sheep painted high on the wall. I move in to look for a flat spot for my sleeping bag. There is a rock as big and flat as a table with another stone leaning against it, flat like a large tile, yet small enough to move. I pick up the small stone and turn it over. A metate, concave from a million seeds ground between it and its mano, the corresponding round, handheld stone. When they moved on, the last people who lived in the alcove left it because it was too heavy to carry. I have read that it was common for nomadic people to turn the metate over and lean it against another rock to minimize erosion so it would remain functional until they returned.

When I need to dream, I go back to that alcove, that moment. Glen and I had both found metates before, but this time it was different. When I turned the metate over, I felt a gush of invisible energy, released at the speed of light. No one had touched that stone for a thousand years. We stared at the metate, knowing in some strange way we couldn't explain that the desert people who migrated through these canyons a thousand years ago had left the stone for us. Although they never came back, we did, Glen and I. We weren't sure what had happened to them. We were sure that we were part of a different world, one much larger than anything we had ever dreamed of before, bigger not just in space but in time. We sat there for what felt like hours while the air seemed filled with nonverbal answers to questions: Where did we come from? Why are we here? Why us? Why now? How do we fit? What is important?

We put the metate back carefully, just as we had found it, for someone else who might need it later.

We brought back in our brains what memories we could of that moment but found ourselves at a loss for words to describe how we felt. We knew, then, that the complete experience was stored somewhere else in our bodies.

Even today, when Glen and I talk about that metate, we whisper.

I learned later that what I had felt while turning over that metate was a "peak experience," as described by psychologist and philosopher Abraham Maslow in his book *Religions, Values, and Peak-Experiences*. Although they don't remember it, my uncle J. D. and my aunt Bea gave me the book when I was still in high school. I remember thanking them but wondering why on earth they thought I would be interested in a book like that. I stored it. Somehow it followed me, box to box, house to house, until I needed it.

According to Maslow, a peak experience involves perceiving the universe as a whole. There is a feeling of belonging, of looking at the world from a higher vantage and seeing a broader picture. Nature is seen as an end in itself, not as a means for human purposes. Self-centeredness dissolves.

Heaven takes on new meaning during a peak experience. No longer a faraway place, it suddenly exists all the time, all around us, and can be entered into briefly. There may be glimpses of eternity.

At the same time, the experience makes the individual more receptive to listening and learning. Life's dichotomies and conflicts tend to dissolve, along with fear and anxiety. Facts and values fuse. Time loses importance. The world seems only good, beautiful, and desirable; evil has a place, but as part of the whole.

To many, the experience is ineffable, difficult to describe. There is an overwhelming feeling of gratitude for having been blessed with a new sense of the sacred.

Some people never have peak experiences. Maslow believed that those committed to an organized religion are less likely to have or to acknowledge having a peak experience. Conversely, those who have had a peak experience have trouble accepting religion into their lives.

In a sense, he said, people who have had a peak experience have their own religion.

Fourteen

A S USUAL, RETURNING TO THE CITY after a weekend in the wilderness was difficult, and the monotonous details that filled me up inside tried to crowd out the wild memories of my trip. Terry had been gone, too, and I came home to bad refrigerator smells and running water from a broken sprinkler. At work, pink notes from Friday screamed about the shower partitions I'd forgotten to order, the flush valves that should have been there but weren't, the stained, stainless steel sinks. Getting away was getting impossible.

By the time I finally escaped to Spring Creek, a remote canyon in Capitol Reef National Park, I had planned and canceled the trip three times. It had been months since I had camped out and two years since I had spent a whole weekend naked. Inwardly, a storm was raging.

Hiking on the first day, I couldn't get my mind off work. I hadn't had a day to myself since becoming Dave Lovell's partner two months earlier. The previous three months had been the most stressful of my life. That was the time between telling my father and brothers that I wanted to phase myself out of the family business and actually doing it. I kept thinking about my family and the implications of my decision to leave the company.

Outwardly, I had been looking for a way to leave without putting more responsibility on the shoulders of my father, who was ready to slow down. After many closed-door meetings, long lunches, pages of notes, thousands of numbers on an adding machine tape the length of a football field, and a little shouting (the first ever heard within those walls), the details were complete. We would split off one division of Rex W. Williams & Sons and sell it to a friendly competitor, the Lovell Company. I would work with Dave Lovell during a three-year transition period beginning on July 1, 1989. My involvement would give Dave time to establish relationships with the manufacturers I would bring to the partnership, and I would have time to think about what the hell to do next.

The process, though painful, was productive. My brothers, my father, and I all dealt with issues we hadn't felt comfortable with before, such as style differences, weird quirks we had, and the church. After one long meeting during which we had all opened up, my father asked me to stay for a minute. "I wonder," he said, "whether I should really be teaching the gospel to other people when I can't get my own son to understand." I told him that I *was* a spiritual person and that he and I weren't on paths going in opposite directions. Still, I was sorry to be the source of some of his guilt.

Besides my camping gear, I carried three quarts of water from home into Spring Creek. Although I have been here for twenty-four hours, I have not found the canyon's namesake, or any other water. I have half a quart left. I am hot enough to sweat while lying in the shade on this flat rock, and I am thirsty.

At first, I think only about water, not wanting to drink the little I have left but feeling parched. But a breeze cools my body, and my mind begins to wander.

I am also desperate to release the pressure inside me. Four generations of Williams men—all growing up in the Mormon Church, all getting married young, having families, all working for the company—had created an inertia of geologic proportions. People say that the men in my family look the same; I'm sure they think we act the same as well.

I feel like a steam locomotive trying to move. The fire has been built, the coal ignited. Out here on this rock, holding on, I can feel the water begin to boil. I know it will take a lot of steam to move this train. Extracting myself from a history of family patterns has made me very tired.

I feel as if I've been skiing up a long traverse and my uphill leg aches. Changing directions and uphill legs will make the pain disappear. I have ignored half of myself, one of my halflives. The other half is exhausted.

"Why have I put myself through this?" I ask the rock.

I envy my brothers and sisters, who never seem to question their roles in life. Becky, the oldest, is curious and smart. As a child, she was a bookworm with a million questions. She became a nurse, though she could have been a doctor. Instead, she married one. Dave is a bighearted plastic surgeon who balances the work he does enhancing breasts by treating burn victims and people with cleft palates in developing countries. They have three children. My little sister, Nan, and her husband, Steve, an art dealer, have five kids. They spend their summers at a mountain cabin. My little brothers, Joe and Tom, are now partners in the family business. Joe has always been the salesman of the family, the promoter. Everyone likes Joe, and his family life seems like a party. They have boats and a cabin and season's ski passes. Tom, the youngest, is intense, the most organized person in the world. His family lives on a strict low-fat diet; they exercise daily. Tom and Joe make a perfect business team. Between them, they have eight kids.

In my family, I am the most different. I am no longer active in the Mormon Church. I don't know exactly why. In part, I think I lack sufficient imagination. For example, I have trouble with the belief that after death, Mormons go to one of three different kingdoms, depending on how worthy they are. The highest kingdom, the Celestial, is reserved for the best of the best—people like my parents and grandparents. People who make it to this kingdom become gods of their own world. The next best go to the Terrestrial, the middle kingdom. At the bottom is the Telestial Kingdom, which, despite its lowly stature, still exceeds anything we will have experienced on earth. I guess I can't imagine anything better or more beautiful than this planet.

I also have a problem with the Mormon belief that spirits of unborn babies wait for a body to inhabit so they can be tested during life to determine which kingdom they'll end up in. I worry that if this earth is seen as a means to some other end, people will abuse it. If I were to make up the test to determine worthiness, I would mandate that people leave this place better than they found it.

Finally, I can't imagine how any one organized religion can claim sole access to the "truth" and can justify spreading missionaries all over the world to teach it, dividing families and infecting other cultures in the process. I could accept Mormonism as a legitimate method of pursuing the truth instead of claiming to have a lock on it. I, for one, am not sure exactly what truth is.

I am sure that my father or my brother Tom could effectively explain the three kingdoms, unborn spirits, earth as a means to an end, and truth—and that they would be more than willing to share their explanations with me if I were open to it. Since I'm not open, I have to acknowledge that there might be deeper, personal, hidden reasons why I haven't been able to embrace Mormonism.

Sometimes I wonder whether I suffer from an undiagnosed childhood brain injury caused by my head being forcibly extracted from between the iron rods in the fence around Brigham Young's grave, where I'd gotten it stuck during a celebration of his birthday. I was eight years old. My dad yanked me free before my screaming completely ruined the mood of the day.

Down deep, I might be blaming the church for my mother's stress and anger when I was young. I'm not sure whether or not the choices she made early in her life were dictated by the church. For whatever reason, she did what the culture expected of her. For example, she gave birth to four children in the first five years of her marriage, a feat she had accomplished by the age of twenty-five. There were times when I knew the stress was too much for her, and I thought we were driving her crazy. The church promotes an image of the perfect woman as an immaculate housekeeper, devoted mother, and dutiful, loving wife. My mother was all that, but it was hard on her. It was hard on all of us.

My father seemed to take it all in stride, as if the travails of a big family and a stressed wife were part of some plan. I don't remember him ever being really angry or frustrated, and not because he isn't emotional. He—like his father—is one of the most consistently happy people I know. He learned at a young age, probably on his mission to Nova Scotia or possibly before, that the Mormon Church was true. He "knew" and did not doubt that Christ had reappeared on our continent after he was crucified in order to give the truth of life to a man named Nephi, who wrote it all down on the Golden Plates, which were found and interpreted centuries later by Joseph Smith. My father has always been totally dedicated to Mormonism, but he's never flaunted his faith, never acted "holier than thou." By the time he was thirty, he had been named bishop of our ward, one of the youngest anyone had ever heard of. He was gone almost every night after work, attending regularly scheduled meetings or helping people who were struggling, oblivious (according to my mother) to the extent to which his own young family needed him. Family folklore has my mother putting a sign saying "Husband Wanted" on the front lawn, where he could see it. I remember looking forward to Thursday nights because I knew he would be staying home with us, buffering us from our angry, perfect mother.

I remember first feeling out of place one Sunday in 1964. I was twelve. I was at a "Farewell," a church meeting to honor a young man who was going on his mission. Almost all Mormon families send their male children on a two-year mission to another part of the world when they turn nineteen. It is customary for the missionary to give a speech at the end of the meeting. I remember this speaker clearly. At one point, he looked right at me when he said that he had waited and prepared for his whole life to go on his mission. He challenged me and the boys sitting near me, telling us that if we would "listen for that still, small voice" and follow it, we could serve our own missions. I was confused. I could hear my "still, small voice," but it wasn't telling me how to prepare for my mission. It was warning me that I had just seven years to get out of it.

Still, I kept going to church. As a young boy, trying to fit in was hard enough without going against a hundred years of family history and a neighborhood where four of the five kids my age went to church. I remember wondering whether everyone felt the way I did and figuring that one day I would understand it and become a committed Mormon. It never happened.

I'm sure my family feels sorry for me, with no children and no testimony (no feeling in my heart that the Mormon Church is the only true religion). At least they've had a long time to adjust to my quirkiness. In fact, they probably think that, based on my history, it makes perfect sense for me to sacrifice financial security by quitting a job that would be the envy of almost anybody else. I know that some family members perceive me as the black sheep, the poor soul who will probably end up with some booby prize in the afterlife.

I prefer to think of myself as the wild potato, after something I read once. During planting season, South American farmers throw a few seed potatoes out in the wild, where they are subject to the random pollinating forces of nature. If a blight or a drought kills the potatoes in their fields, the farmers can go out in the wild to find the survivors and use them for seed. I am the wild potato in my family. If anything in their lives or religion goes wrong or falls apart, my family can find me out there in the wild, and maybe I can help. To my mind, it is lucky for them that I am different.

I am lucky that they are who they are. It creates a kind of stasis. We know who and what we can count on. I know that any struggles we had while growing up—with our father working so hard and going to all those meetings and our mother burdened with the responsibility of raising five kids—weren't serious and only because our parents desperately loved us and wanted nothing but the best for us.

The cottonwood in the middle of the dry wash shades my rock, and I can stare directly at the sun without squinting by looking up through the filter of leaves. The roots of the giant tree spread out in all directions, holding the rock and sand together. A rock wall in every shade from white to red stands behind me. The river that once ran in front of me has been gone since spring, reduced to brick-hard mud marred by the tracks of a tree frog and a collared lizard who have sucked up the water I can't have. I look into the future, and for the first time in my life I can't find anything familiar. I need water, but I am so comfortable sitting here, dappled shadows dancing on my bare skin, that I will seriously consider dying of thirst before I move.

When I was growing up, my parents always made me feel important, and this gave me confidence. They took my school projects very seriously and rarely missed my baseball games. Later, my wilderness forays always seemed to fascinate them. My mother loved to help plan my trips and wanted to talk about them in great detail when I got home. Once, Hink and I spent three weeks traveling through Washington—the Olympic rain forest, the Cascade Range. I promised my mother I'd call every Sunday, and I did. On the second Sunday, I called to let her know that we were fine and had just climbed Mount Rainier. "I wish you'd told me before," she said, "so I could have worried."

In 1982, my mother's heart broke, literally. She didn't have a heart attack, but she would have, had she not had immediate coronary bypass surgery. At fifty-one, she was too young to have a bad heart, the doctors said, mystified by her condition, but they didn't know her past or anything about the toll that fear and abuse take on very young hearts. After her surgery, she totally changed her life. She ate better and walked hard every day. She learned her limits and didn't let anyone pressure her into doing anything stressful. She learned to say no. She began spending hours every week talking to confused young mothers who always felt like crying even though they were doing every-thing they thought was right.

Still, underneath it all, in a silent part of her, a clock ticked. In five years, the doctors said, she'd be in again.

Together, my parents had the entire spectrum covered. My mother encouraged me to experience life, day to day. My dad has always felt responsible for my future, both temporal and spiritual.

Success, we were taught, involved "tunnel vision"—focusing on one goal, one end point in life. We learned an important les-son about success and being focused every time Grandpa Bran-dley took us to the west desert to look for topaz. To find this quartzlike mineral, he had us lean against the car and look out over the desert until a ray of sun hit an individual piece that was perfectly positioned to reflect the ray back into our eyes. We then memorized the exact point and began walking toward it, whether it was a hundred yards or a mile away. We were instructed not to take our eyes off that point under any circum-stances, even if we were to hear a snake in the sand. When we reached our point of focus, the topaz was always there. One day, I found four good pieces by using my grandfather's technique, but when I think back on it I wonder what birds I missed, or col-ors, or animal tracks. Sometimes I wonder whether I have avoided commonly held visions of success because of the early goal setting it required. Did I know that being too focused on future goals can obliterate unexpected experiences? And what about the fear of spending a lifetime in pursuit of a goal only to attain it and find that it is not what I expected? What if the shining object turns out to be not topaz but a Budweiser can?

The sun moves in the sky, silently robbing me of shade. The heat sharpens and stabs me, and I need to decide soon either to leave for the car with the half quart of water I have left or to stay and search farther upstream for a stagnant pool, a wet place to dig, a shaded pothole, or—imagine—a spring.

Why does it seem that in the desert, decisions are cut and dried, black and white, involving two choices—one that works and one that doesn't? Unlike the plumbing business, where for every question there are as many answers as there is time to consider the question. None completely right or completely wrong; just different stages of inconsistency.

I get down from my rock, leaving a body-sized wet spot on the sandstone. I pee into the sand, stretching my arms and flexing my muscles and not holding myself, not needing to aim. I am relieved to see that my urine is still light yellow; I know I am safe for a while. If I don't drink, my urine will darken before it turns orange and then shuts off all together, the day before I die.

I think about the water I wasted two weeks earlier at a trade show, where I was demonstrating a toilet that flushes on just a gallon and a half. The drain didn't work, and I spilled five gallons on the floor of the convention center. Or the hundreds of gallons my automatic sprinkler system back home empties every other day to keep my grass green. Or the millions of daily showers we take in America because we are afraid of how we might smell if we didn't.

I walk upstream, looking for water. Although the canyon becomes tighter and fills with shade, sweat still drips from my pores. I wonder what I know in my cells about finding water. Does something deep inside me know how? Which animals to watch. The smell or feel of the air. If it were a matter of life or death, would there be some external tug on the many gallons of water making up my body? Or are humans so removed from nature because of faucets and pipes that this ability, this cellular memory, has become obsolete? What else inside us have we forgotten how to use?

Nothing moves, and there are no sounds. I dig a hole in the mud with a stick, hoping it will fill, but it doesn't. I check every old pool lined with cracked mud like peeling red paint. I follow a flying beetle, thinking it might need water and lead me to some. Nothing. I hurry back to the rock and pick up my pack.

They say a thirsty hiker should carry in his stomach any water he has left in case dehydration becomes severe enough to addle his brain, making him forget to drink. Although I'm far from being seriously dehydrated, I drink what is left in my bottle. Immediately, my cells blossom and I feel free—the freedom of having no more choices to make. Then I start across four miles of huge, wide desert. The temperature is 100+ degrees Fahrenheit, and the sun's intensity threatens to burn holes in my hat.

Rock monoliths the shape and size of castles mark the way. My footprints from before are barely visible in the hard sand. Across the expanse, I can see the break in the cliff I need to climb to get to my truck, which sits baking in the sun. I stop once to put on my clothes after pressing on my hip and finding a white fingerprint on my tomato-colored skin. Then I lapse into a rhythm. The clothes feel foreign, but I flow like the missing river, sweat dripping off the end of my nose. Judging by his tracks in the sand, a small coyote is hours ahead of me. I can hear the quick gasps of ravens' wings and see their shadows cross my path, but when I look up I see only the sun's massive glare. There is no other sound.

I reach the top of the cliff and drop my pack. I pull out my empty water bottle and fill it from the jug in my car. Then I turn around and look all the way back to Spring Creek, past the sandstone castles, the expanse, past my family and the heart of my mother, past the turns in the dry river and the shadow of cottonwood and raven, all the way back to "Why have I put myself through this," the original question, which no longer seems significant.

I take a good, long drink. The water is hot. But because there is nothing else, it tastes like tea. It tastes good.

PART III

Flesh

From the sketch to the work, one travels on one's knees.

—Vladamir Holan, quoted by Milan Kundera
in *The Art of the Novel*

Fifteen

I N 1992, THE MONTH OF APRIL seemed endless. When the last
weekend finally arrived, Terry and I escaped, driving to
Moab to search unnamed canyons for pictographs and petroglyphs. We needed to relax because we were both exhausted.
She had been traveling for most of the month, and I had been
through the most intense period of my life. I tried to piece it all
together as we drove south.

First, my friend Hink was very sick. He'd been skiing when
a massive headache suddenly attacked him. Within hours, he
was in a coma that would last ten days. I heard about it a day
later and called Annie, his wife, who was understandably dis-
traught. No one could give her a diagnosis or tell her why this
had happened. When he came to, they packed up their two children and flew to Salt Lake City, where there were doctors who
knew more about brains than they did in Alaska.

The doctors quickly eliminated the obvious reasons—
tumor, stroke, etc. But when they injected a dye through a
hole in Hink's head, the same thing happened. He stayed
down a week this time. When he woke up, he looked terrible.
They'd shaved half his head and he was very skinny, not the
robust Hink whose strength and endurance had always

inspired me. I couldn't believe what I saw and couldn't say anything. The family went home to Alaska in December. In February, a friend called to say that Hink had been on his roof shoveling snow when he'd suddenly fallen off. He was in his third coma. I couldn't deal with the news, so I put it out of my mind. Looking back, I guess I had always seen Hink as a pillar of strength, someone I totally trusted and could depend on in any situation. I didn't want any other vision of him. I didn't call.

I'm not sure what changed, but in early April I called. Annie answered. I told her that I was sorry for not calling sooner, that I was having a difficult time dealing with Hink's illness. But I also said that I knew I'd been selfish because as difficult a time as I was having, I knew it was a million times worse for her. She said she understood; I'll always love her for her empathy. She then told me she had spent months researching the brain, but still no one had an explanation for Hink's "lights going out."

She said the two of them had reassessed their lives and decided that being together as a family was more important than working all the time to make money to buy things they didn't have time to use anyway.

"Do you want to talk to him?" she asked. I was surprised to hear that he was home.

"Sure," I said. "Is it all right?"

"He would love to talk to you."

I waited a minute while Hink came to the phone. I was scared, not knowing what to expect. When he got on, there was a second or two delay before he responded to what I said. The delay reminded me of the days before fiber optics when I would call Hink in Alaska and have to wait for the sound to travel through the wires. This time, the delay was not caused by the cable; rather, it took a second or two for what I said to register in Hink's injured brain. But what he said will always stay with me. "My priorities have been mixed up," he said. "No matter what they find, I know this is my body's way of telling me to slow down. Enjoy life. I'm in the process of making some real changes."

Before we hung up, Hink suggested a sea kayak trip in Kenai Fjords. "Not this summer," he said. "I won't be ready. But next year. For sure."

"For sure," I said.

That same month, I decided to leave the Lovell Company. When Dave and I had formed our partnership, we'd agreed that our contract would dissolve three years later, on June 30. During that time, I intended to work with Dave and save some money while planning my new career, but it didn't work out that way.

Dave and I had a great time working together. He loves the business more than I thought possible, and next to his family, it is what he cares most about. He and I spent hours each week developing strategies as if the world would come apart if we didn't get products to our customers. Dave was better than I was with wholesalers; my strength was in working with architects and engineers. People in the industry were amazed at what a good team we were. Dave worked all the time. For him, Sundays were the same as any other day except that he took his shoes off at the office. Toward the end, I couldn't keep my other halflife fed and keep up with him at the same time.

When our contract was two months from expiration, Dave came into my office and asked whether I wanted to extend it. Without thinking about the future or about security or Terry, I blurted out something I wasn't even sure I believed. I said no—no more contract. And I quit. At first, I wanted to suck back those words. I couldn't believe what I had heard myself say. But by the smile on Dave's face and how I felt, I knew my decision was right. I felt as if I had jumped into a pond without knowing the temperature and was shocked that it felt so good.

Heading south, Terry and I were both quiet. I wondered to what extent Hink's illness had inspired me to give up a fifteen-year career and swerve off onto a new, unknown path. I was also haunted by the scene I'd created earlier in the week, on my fortieth birthday.

Terry had surprised me that day with a tree—a thundering plum with beautiful purple leaves and pinking buds. The man from the nursery offered to plant it and suggested a few spots in our yard where it would probably thrive. Terry and I couldn't agree on the perfect spot. After the nurseryman and I had picked up the bucket containing the 200-pound tree and its roots and moved it to its twelfth new location, I was tired and I was mad. I didn't realize how much I had bottled up inside. "Look. Thanks. You can go. I'll plant it myself," I said to the man while trying to contain my temper. After he left, when Terry and I were alone, I lost it.

"This is my tree, you gave it to me, and I will plant it wherever the hell I want it!" Terry gave me that look only a wife can give, letting me know I was out of line. Then she left. I sat alone with the tree for half an hour before deciding on a spot where I could see it from my favorite chair. I spent the remaining daylight hours alone, digging a hole three feet deep and two feet across, and finally planted the tree where I wanted it.

Terry and I didn't speak much for the rest of the evening.

While driving south to Moab, we talk about the thundering plum. We can laugh about it now. Although it sometimes makes me mad when she does it, Terry is good at looking at what angers me from a point just beneath the surface. Before we reach Moab, I decide that the tree is symbolic of me and my emotional turmoil. I didn't want to be planted until I was sure where I needed to be, and I certainly didn't want a committee telling me where to go and what to do.

It is dark when we pull into Glen's driveway. He is out of town, but we know where to find the key.

The next morning, we drive another hour south to Canyonlands National Park. Our first stop is Newspaper Rock, where sometime in the past two thousand years, thousands of figures were carved into the desert varnish that formed when oxides from above leached through the rock. Bison, deer, snakes, and hundreds of unrecognizable figures cover a wall the size of a movie screen. Rock art archaeologists believe that Newspaper Rock was on a major trade route and everyone passing this point stopped to tell his or her story. I believe that Newspaper Rock has always been a sacred place, part of a pilgrimage, because that is what I feel every time I visit.

Before getting back in the car, we stop at the tables where Navajo Indians are selling their wares. I glance past the beadwork and small baskets to the silver jewelry. I find a simple silver band, and slip it on my ring finger. It is too big, so I shift it to my middle finger. Terry notices what I am doing.

"That's nice. Why don't you buy it?"

"I don't like rings."

"Then why are you trying it on?"

"I'm not sure."

"Maybe you really do want a wedding ring. That business about 'the smile on your face' is wearing a little thin." She grinned.

Lately I'd begun to complain about marriage and how, after a few years, insignificant details tend to take up all the space and suck in all the air—things like lightbulbs and lawns, places that get missed while shaving, and who cooks and who takes out the trash. Two months earlier, my frustration had come to a head when Terry left for ten days during a particularly stressful time for me and I was feeling sorry for myself.

"I only get bones," I had said when she returned.

The next morning, we had driven out to Great Salt Lake to ceremonially dissolve our marriage. We figured that if we could clear away enough of the bullshit, we might see the real reason why we are together. It was like rubbing tarnish off silver. It was a good thing to do.

From Terry's perspective, my working all the time made it easy for me to mask our problems. Great chunks of me had become off-limits to her. When I did get outdoors, she wasn't included. I deliberately sought risky ski routes and long, lonely runs. I couldn't see that my halflives were spreading farther apart and that leaping between them was becoming more and more difficult.

One night, I picked up Wendell Berry's book *Home Economics* and noticed a line that Terry had underlined and written a small *b* next to: " . . . that it must always be necessary to suffer at work in order to enjoy ourselves in places specializing in 'recreation.'" I knew her note meant that this passage applied to me and helped explain me to her. At first, it made me mad, not wanting to admit that my life was out of balance. I wondered whether balance would be easier if I were happy in my work.

I buy the ring. It costs eight dollars.

Late the next morning, we have driven to the lip of Horse-shoe Canyon, a small, LEGO®-shaped area detached from, yet part of, Canyonlands National Park. It is included in the park because of its rock art panels. We have come to see the most famous, the Great Gallery. Neither of us has been here before.

Loaded up with water and food, we start down the well-marked trail about noon. All along the way, hikers struggle upward in the heat. They are sweating, but they say that what they have seen is worth their effort. We move downhill along a pink slickrock trail, as effortlessly as poured liquid, to the bottom. Just-heated air rushes up the canyon walls, and moves our hair.

We reach the canyon floor in an hour. We walk silently and quickly with our eyes up and darting side to side, afraid to miss anything. A pair of ravens flies past us and lands, waits for us to pass, and then flies ahead, landing again. Ravens mate for life.

Finally, at four o'clock we make one last turn around a river bend, and in front of us, as if in a dream, red life-sized figures stare out from beyond a cottonwood tree. We scramble up the loose sand bank and into the cliff shade. Above and curving to our right and our left for the length of an outdoor movie screen, the Great Gallery surrounds us. Terry drops to her knees, and I suck in a long breath and hold onto it for a minute. Nothing could have prepared us for the large colored figures, the small detailed ones, the numbers and sizes of them. Nothing about them is familiar; we feel some foreign existence where artists work in other dimensions. It is like being part of someone else's dream. There are too many figures to count, some coming, some going, as if the rock wall were a permeable membrane between worlds. The longer we stand still, the more figures appear. Up high, the light releases smaller ones that hurtle my imagination.

One figure, my size, has a framelike body outlined with red paint splattered in lines. Its ghostlike head, with ovoid eyes defined by their absence, stares out from the middle of time. With its large shoulders and tilted presence, the image seems to float next to the wall. It is surrounded by tall, dark presences drawn in three dimensions, maybe more.

We realize that we are standing on a perfectly flat platform at the base of the wall—a place to dance, so we do. We can't help ourselves.

We move along the ledge until we come upon a great mother figure draped in purple. She has a bird on each shoulder: white on one, dark on the other, as if to balance good and evil. We are dead quiet. We forget to breathe.

"This is as wild and sacred a place as I've ever been."

"I know. I feel it." We whisper.

"After we dissolved our marriage, we never replaced it with anything," Terry says, slipping her hand into mine. "We never made new vows. I think we need to."

She is right. The Great Gallery is the perfect place for renewed commitments. We think about new vows for a moment.

I couldn't tell which one of us said what, but with our words braiding together, forming a cord between us, we redefined our marriage there beneath the Great Gallery. We changed it from something precise, with a socially acceptable definition like a fence containing us, to a vehicle for change not only in our own lives but also for change in the world. A vehicle to hold us, a place with dimension, a moving place to ride—and hide in if we need to—as we travel along our own paths toward preserving what we find sacred in the world. We stood there below our ancient witnesses, holding each other for a long time.

Walking out seemed faster; we had a rhythm that turned hypnotic. I felt good. I thought about the vows, wanting them to last for a while.

As the sun dropped below the cliff, we walked up the long, steep path out of the canyon, into the shade. I thought about work—not my job but work as in carrying a pack up a hill. Force times distance, real work. No one was around when we got to the top.

The sky looked as if someone had smashed the sun and smeared its color the full length of the horizon. We had a long way to drive, but the sky had that mother-of-pearl feeling that, no matter how big a hurry I'm in, I want to stop, lean against something, and just look for a while, which is exactly what we did.

We had 300 miles to go, 40 of them on a dirt road. It is a good dirt road—you can go 50 miles per hour—and in the low light, the green hills looked deep and beautiful. We didn't talk much once we reached the highway, but watched as the scenery seemed to float by on boats. I felt as if we'd just made love.

It was past midnight when we pulled into our driveway. I bowed my back to stretch it and breathed in some spring. Inside, bone tired, I dumped an armload of gear in the empty

guest room. As I turned to leave, I noticed a hand-colored photograph hanging on the east wall. The image, framed in pewter,
had hung in full view for three years, but I hadn't paid it much
attention.

Titled *The Holy Ghost,* it was a photograph of the haunting
red figure Terry and I had stared at for twenty minutes at the
Great Gallery that afternoon—the framelike figure with the
glaring, ovoid eyes. Sure, the photographer's hand-tinting had
changed the colors slightly, but the figure was unmistakable.
Oddly, though, while standing there in the canyon surrounded
by rock and the Holy Ghost, my bare feet lost in the sand, I had
not recognized it as the photograph on our wall.

I remember reading that images need knowledge or a social
context for intelligent interpretation. The only knowledge we
had when we hung the image on our wall was that it was rock
art, probably painted on sandstone somewhere on the Colorado
Plateau, and that we both thought it was beautiful. But being
there in Horseshoe Canyon had somehow released the image,
letting it run wild in my mind.

Perhaps movement helped free the image. Whenever I had
looked carefully at the photograph on the wall, I'd been static,
like a statue. In the canyon, we were moving all day—down
through the cliffs, along the wash, dancing there in front of the
figure. We had seen the figure's rocky texture up close and seen
the decorations incised into its body. We had moved back, to
test its size, and then right and left as its eyes seemed to follow
us. The image demanded to be seen from all directions. Deep
ecologist Dolores LaChappelle wrote, "As the human body
moves through the landscape certain things happen, which
enable seeing," and I believe her.

In the canyon, we had been mesmerized by the context.

Whereas the height and width of the pewter frame define the picture on our wall, our seeing the figure in the desert in context with the others—moving among them, touching the textures on the wall, comparing the figure's size with our own, hearing the breeze and rattle of cottonwood leaves—gave us added knowledge. If art is the relationship between object and observer, then that night, as the observer, I was better at holding up my end.

Standing there in the guest room, tired and looking at the picture as if it were a hole through the center of my life, there was something I wanted to remember. There is the figure painted and scratched onto the sandstone, and then there is the photographic image of the figure. But there is more. The figure we stood before in Horseshoe Canyon was also an image painted by a primitive artist, a representation of something real and powerful that I've tried hard to imagine.

Looking down, I noticed another picture standing on top of the bookcase, a framed photograph of Terry and me on our wedding day.

Since then, I've spent more time looking at the picture of the rock ghost and the picture of our wedding. I'm comfortable seeing them both as images of real things, symbols, just as a heart symbolizes love, with different meanings for everyone who sees them. The rock art picture takes me back to that whole day in the canyon—to something big and out of this world yet real and powerful and so complicated that I may never fully understand it. Just like marriage. Our wedding picture shows a couple of children on the happiest day of their lives. The image symbolizes only the word *marriage,* not the idea. Not the ache or the possibility.

The poet W. S. Merwin said that paying attention is not as

important as attention itself. I think he meant that attention alone is an end in itself—it is a state of being. Attention to rock art goes beyond wondering what it means or forcing it to send a message from its world to ours. Maybe attention is what made us dance so spontaneously in the canyon instead of thinking and analyzing. Is it the same with marriage? Are we to analyze it, focus it, make it fit inside a frame and match the static vision of eternal happiness and youth the world tries to sell us? Or dance? It sounds so simple. What makes it so hard?

Sixteen

I SPENT THE LAST THREE DAYS OF JUNE cleaning out my office at the Lovell Company. The task would have gone more quickly if I had thrown everything away. Instead, I spent hours carefully dividing the contents into three piles: significant trivia (interesting memorabilia I had kept through the years), library (information on products someone might need someday), and garbage. I threw out the garbage and then, deciding it had no value to anyone but me, threw out my library.

I went through the trivia pile piece by piece. Many of the items took me on long memory rides back through the years. I found a photograph of Terry and me that was encased in a plastic key chain. We were sitting in a restaurant in Freeport, Bahamas, on a trip I'd won by meeting my sales quota for water coolers. I remembered what a beautiful place it was but what a difficult time we'd had escaping the plumbing supply salesmen and their wives to find the real island. Even the beach had been fenced to separate the natives from the tourists.

I found a program from a plumbing convention in Jackson Hole, Wyoming. Terry and I were listed as hosting an early morning bird walk. Besides attending product and insurance seminars, the men had been scheduled to play golf. The women could choose among flower arranging, Color Me Beautiful workshops, and wok cooking classes. Only one plumber showed up for our bird walk, and then, he said, only because he "couldn't sleep and wondered what kind of people get up that early to look for birds they can't shoot."

I found a copy of the keynote speech given at a Bradley sales meeting by Al McGuire, the famous Marquette University basketball coach. In it, Coach McGuire told a story of ordering lobster in a nice restaurant. When the waiter brought it out, his lobster was missing one claw, and McGuire wanted to know why. The waiter told him that the lobsters came to the restaurant alive and were put into a big tank, where they often fought. "Take this back," McGuire had told the waiter, "and bring me a winner."

Then I threw the trivia pile away. Even the key chain.

I quit with enough money to live for a year, an individual retirement account, and a used Ford Explorer. I hoped that within that year, I would find something new. I wanted to do something I believed in *and* get paid for it. I wanted a job with an environmental slant but one with flexibility. I had the feeling that if I found the right niche, flexibility wouldn't matter. Ideally, I wanted to work and play and not know the difference.

A year earlier, I had written a magazine piece about how economic concerns were driving environmental issues. In it, I repeated a story I'd overheard in a café in Green River, Utah, a few days after plans had been announced for construction of a nuclear waste incinerator there. Part of the conversation went like this:

"Have you heard about the nuclear plant?"

"You mean the jobs. There'll be a ton of them."

"But nuclear waste coming in from all over—doesn't that worry you?"

"No way. With all the goddamn regulations, they'll have that stuff packed perfectly. You can bet on that."

"God, we need the work."

Back home, I did some research and found that, at the time, unemployment in Green River was at 21 percent. I wondered how a conversation among those same three people might have differed had unemployment been, say, only 10 percent.

"Have you heard about the nuclear plant?"

"That thing—it'll never fly."

"Over my dead body will we let them burn that shit here. What do they think we are, the toilet bowl of the world?"

"Can you imagine what that waste would do to our melons?"

Then I outlined a fictional scenario about Escalante, which is a southern Utah town populated by fewer than 1,000 people and surrounded by large tracts of wilderness, the protection of which is being blamed for the town's economic woes. I imagined that two local people opened a small factory, where they made hiking shoes. The idea was that locals wouldn't look with such disdain on hikers who supported wilderness preservation and visited the area wearing shoes made by Escalantans. I suppose I made a powerful case because The Nature Conservancy in Utah contacted me to ask whether I thought my scenario was actually possible. They even offered to pay me to study the idea further. I agreed, had some business cards printed, and suddenly found myself in business as a consultant.

My friend Doug Peacock read my story, too, and sent a nice card. "Maybe this is a way of saving some of it," he said. Doug is a writer who spends most of his time looking for grizzly bears in Montana or wandering in southwestern deserts. I was surprised by his tone. After years of being involved in preservation issues, I saw people as fitting into two categories: those whose lives have no room for words, compromise, and consensus and those who look for common ground, ways to bring opposing poles together to work things out. I call those in the first group warriors and those in the second peacemakers. The success of the movement, I believe, depends on both.

Peacock is a warrior. I am in the second category, not because I disagree with the warriors but because I'm a former salesman and something in me thinks that with enough work and information, most problems can be solved.

I remember reading the introduction to Nikos Kazantzakis's epic poem *The Odyssey: A Modern Sequel* the month I quit my job:

> A man has three duties. His first duty is to the mind which imposes order on disorder. . . . But his second duty is to the heart, which admits of no boundaries. . . . His third duty is to free himself of both mind and heart, from the great temptation of hope.

I concluded that beyond our personal thoughts and feelings lies a way to live that works, a balanced place where personal clarity is more important than victory.

I wanted to explore the third duty and search for that place.

So, nearly a year to the day since I had declared my freedom from the plumbing industry, I was in Escalante under contract with the Governor's Office of Planning and Budget, testing some of the theories I'd developed with The Nature Conservancy. I needed to document real obstacles rural people face in starting sustainable businesses. I got the contract because they liked my work experience and my creative approach to the preservation problems that had plagued the state for years. Other than that, I had absolutely no business being involved in rural economic development.

I saw locally owned businesses as one way these communities could guide their own future, without depending on multinational companies that extract the limited natural resources and show little allegiance to the local workers they hire. My theory is that rural people will take care of the wild places surrounding them if preservation doesn't limit their ability to make a decent living.

On one trip to Escalante, feeling frugal, I decided to camp rather than stay in a motel. (Some say that staying in a motel in Escalante *is* camping.) The weather was way too hot for so early in the year and after two meetings in town and a three-hour walk looking for a road in a remote canyon—I didn't find it, which turned out to be good, since roads disqualify an area from consideration for Wilderness designation—I loaded my pack and wandered down a steep trail to a shaded ledge above a deep, green pool. I swam and read, ate a sandwich when I became hungry, and then climbed into my sleeping bag when I got chilled.

As the sun drops from the sky, I recall Peacock's story in the anthology *Counting Sheep*, compiled by Gary Paul Nabhan. In it, he describes the soporific qualities of a small fire. I rarely build fires, but tonight I will, a very small one, according to the rules Peacock follows on his long, lonely winter hikes in the Sonoran Desert: on sand, with dense wood that burns hot enough to turn to ashes that will blow away to nothing in the slightest breeze.

I stack the broken-pencil-sized oak and juniper sticks I can gather from my bed in a six-inch pile.

I learn that three sips (or were they gulps?) from a pint bottle of Jack Daniels whiskey (Peacock calls it Jack Damage) change this rock-and-raven world to a scene from *Star Wars*. That there is a perfect temperature at which skin and air meet and neither feels neither and they mesh. And that the heat from a small fire is different from the heat of the afternoon sun: fire somehow heats from the inside out; the sun, from the outside in.

I think a lot about Peacock and the way he keeps track of me. I remember some of the conversations we've had: About women, not our wives ("Just this," he said: "You don't want to blow up your life."). About cooking a Thanksgiving turkey ("The best way? OK. First, dig a big, deep hole in your yard. . . ."). About going to coastal Alaska ("You take some tackle in case you get lost and run out of food, a hand line, and a colored lure. A crab pot. You have a crab pot, don't you?" and "Don't take snails from above the low tide line; they can be nasty.").

Peacock and I cross paths regularly, at least twice a year, when he and his family stay at our house on their migration from Tucson, Arizona, through Salt Lake City in early summer and back again in fall.

One year, Peacock called to tell me they would be staying in Heber City instead.

"Why Heber?"

"I need to see a bear."

"A bear? In Heber?"

"Ursus arctos middendorffi. Not grizzly, but almost."

Peacock was referring to Bart, a Kodiak bear who lives in a cage east of Heber. Bart is part of Wasatch Wildlife, a company owned by Doug Seus, an animal trainer who leases wild animals for movies and commercials. Bart was already a celebrity, having starred in the 1989 movie *The Bear.*

For Peacock, bears—their image and mythology, the pure possibility of coming face to face with one in Montana's backcountry—represent all that is real and the limit of what is important. For him, bears epitomize hope wrapped in thick fat and soft fur. They are a source of strength and power.

Peacock sees saving grizzly bears, which are teetering precariously on the thin edge of extinction, as our biggest test. Losing the last American grizzlies means giving way to a weaker, paler version of ourselves. Peacock believes that if we can save the grizzly, we might save ourselves.

I agreed to meet Peacock in Heber City. On the appointed day, I drove through an open gate into a yard full of cages: cougars, black bears, wolves, a raccoon, and a pacing fox. Peacock and Seus were in back, feeding Bart. They were speaking softly as the furry mountain devoured a tubful of thawing chickens Seus had bought at a salvage sale after a train wreck. Peacock and Seus didn't see me, but Bart did, and he exhaled sharply three times before inhaling. I learned later that most bear experts interpret this as a sign of aggression. Peacock and Seus turned around.

"I think Bart is reacting to Brooke," Peacock said, "blowing moisture on his own scent to make it more vivid. I don't *think* he's being aggressive—just curious." I'd learned that Peacock is never sure of anything when it comes to other species. He knows that the most dangerous bears are those a man thinks he understands and that expectations about bears can lead to disaster.

Much has been written about Doug Peacock and his intimacy with bears: how he has lived among them, eating huckleberries and watching them play through his binoculars and camera lenses. Yet seeing Peacock and Bart standing three feet apart from each other, I believed I was witnessing something unique. Peacock's attention turned the air electric, like what driving under high-tension power lines does to a car radio. Seus spoke, and I am sure that Peacock was listening, but he didn't answer. He just stood there face to face with Bart, as if he were looking in a mirror for the first time. I had read in John Reader's book *Man on Earth* that some Native American people believe that people and animals differ only in their outward forms; inside, we are all the same, sharing spirits. Watching Peacock and Bart, I believed that.

Some people speculate that humans have always been fascinated by bears because we are so similar to them. Both species love sweets. Both snore and have good and bad, playful and depressed moods. Bears, like humans, discipline their young yet show undying affection. In fact, Peacock thinks that if humans are special at all, it is because we are bearlike.

The last time I'd seen Peacock was right after Christmas. He and his family had met Terry and me in Moab, where we all stayed in a house south of town. We had a great time walking, eating elaborate meals—turkey and pasta with wild, garlicky sauces—and playing Ping-Pong, which was most memorable for the fact that because all the paddles were broken, we used books.

During the first game, Peacock used his own book, *Grizzly Years,* for a paddle and I used Terry's book *Refuge,* which I traded quickly for *The Ninemile Wolves* by Rick Bass because it weighed less and its cover had a certain texture to it, giving me some real spin on the ball. Peacock, a better player, lost the first two games. We traded "paddles," and I lost the next two. We agreed that the paddle made a difference.

"Too many words," Peacock said about *Grizzly Years*. "I always knew that book had too goddamn many words."

Although Ping-Pong players might agree with him, readers would not. His writing is spare, but he always wants it more so. "Too many words" is Peacock's chief complaint about writing.

Peacock believes that if the story is good, a writer doesn't need many words to tell it, just a few to guide readers along, lodestars to keep them on the trail. Landmarks or cairns. Points of reference. If the story has been told too much, the path becomes worn and boring. So some writers use more and fancier words to confuse readers into believing that the story they are reading is unique. Also, it seems, too many writers are so seduced by their own words that they forget the story, forget they need a story.

My fire's middle glow seems to color the air orange a foot around it, pulsating with the night's sporadic breezes. I lie on my back, watching stars through my binoculars: stars giving birth to more stars as the light dims from my dying fire, the heart in my hands beating, making the stars dance. I see one falling star, and for the first time in my life, I have nothing to wish for.

Little do I know that less than six months later, I will desperately want that wish back.

Seventeen

B Y THE NEXT FEBRUARY, the novelty of my own path was wearing thin. My work wasn't supporting me, and the noise about worth and success being measured in dollars was getting louder. I imagined weird looks from people who mattered. I kept trying to get beyond my mind and heart. But some days, I couldn't even get to heart, stuck in a mind that had turned to mud. For the first time in my life, I was grappling with financial insecurity, which was overtaking me like an infection.

I applied for three jobs to support my vision rather than ignore it, but I didn't get hired. (One employer called to say he was sorry to say they hadn't picked me, but he wanted me to know how entertaining my interview had been.) I realized that without a graduate degree and professional experience in the nonprofit world, or a background in rural economics or environmental issues, I was unemployable. I was so discouraged that I began to think about going back to the plumbing industry. Could I really be that desperate? I yelled at Terry because I was tired of yelling at the mirror.

Regardless of the hours I spent in my office, I didn't have a job, and people began wondering out loud what I was doing. "Do you have any prospects?" they'd ask. I finally called Doug

Peacock, who has never been afraid to admit to being depressed and is good to talk to because he's been down a lot further than I ever have.

Grizzly Years tells the story of Peacock's experiences as a Green Beret medic in Vietnam. He describes numerous brushes with death, too many dead children, and the experience of slowly slipping off the deep end toward insanity. By the time he was sent home, he had been drugged by death and had such a large, rock-hard lump in his throat that he could barely speak. He bought a Jeep and drove west, spending summers in the Rocky Mountains with bears and winters in the southwestern deserts. He wouldn't sleep in a bed for three years.

"Sounds like seasonal affective disorder," Peacock told me on the telephone. "I know it. It happens to me every year, but bad, since I'm 'maniac'-depressive," he said. "You haven't quit talking, obviously. Have you considered crimes of passion or shot any phone booths? No? You've got a long way to go."

"Let's go to Mexico," he said. "There's more light down there, and I need to get some work done." Peacock knows that healing requires living on a real level of life, one at which nothing is right or wrong and there is no expectation or hope, only attention.

Two weeks later, Bob Helmes, a professional desert guide, and I loaded up my truck with all the camping gear we would need in Mexico. We headed south for Tucson, where Peacock lives and where we would also meet up with Rick Bass, a writer from Montana. I needed some perspective—two weeks to sort out my life without the pressure to prove that my decision to switch careers had been the right one. Besides sharing a love of wild places, the four of us had all avoided following a traditional path through life. Bass had been a well-paid oil field geologist before he tossed aside his career to become a writer. Both Bob and I had been salesmen—Hallmark cards and plumbing fixtures, respectively. I'm not sure whether Peacock had held a steady job. Not since I'd known him, anyway.

After fourteen hours on the road and nonstop conversation, Bob and I arrived at Peacock's place on the edge of Tucson. Urban sprawl is a serious problem in Tucson, which is spreading across the desert with alarming speed. I liken it to dough being rolled into a piecrust. With each pass of the rolling pin, the city spreads out farther, with less and less depth. It won't be long before Peacock's place loses the rural feeling it has now.

Inside, Peacock's house had changed since my last visit, three years earlier. He had turned the garage into a nice office, complete with fax machine, computer, and some potsherds tastefully inlaid around the windowsills. Peacock had done the work himself during a serious bout of writer's block. Lisa Peacock seemed happy, and I wondered whether her mood had anything to do with her husband's pending departure. Before going to sleep, I found a petrified cave bear tooth Peacock kept on a bookshelf.

The next morning, we drove to the map store, only to find it closed. I felt nervous about traveling in a new place without a map, but Peacock reassured me. "Look," he said, "we're talking about only three things. Sand and giant lava and somewhere beyond all that, an ocean. Simple." He grinned. I felt better. Next stop, Mexico.

We drove past thousands of square miles of perfectly spaced brittlebrush and creosote. We passed through Organ Pipe Cactus National Monument and then Why, not the question but the junction, twelve miles from the border town of Ajo, Arizona. Then we passed more creosote on our way to Sonoita, Mexico, a beautiful town with clay pots and statues lining its sidewalks. A dark-eyed boy had his bicycle basket filled with giant, hot tortillas folded like bedsheets. We bought three. As we traveled southwest along Highway 8, beautiful miniature monuments marked the dangerous curves where the spirits of unlucky Mexicans had left their bodies during car wrecks. The Pinacate Crater, a massive lava cone, dominated the view from the passenger window for most of the sixty miles to Puerto Peñasco. Then we turned onto a road running due north of town through deep sand along the edge of the Gulf of California. A tilted-up giant whale skull served as a gateway; we slid through it as though drawn by gravity into a deep, wild hole.

We camped that night on a mudflat, well short of our goal. Our plan—and there was little reason to talk about it because it had mostly evaporated, which in Mexico is typical for any plan—had been to leave Peacock's truck many miles north of there at Bahía Adair in the Upper Gulf Biosphere Reserve, near the tip of the Gulf of California. We had planned to take my truck back and leave it at the edge of the massive lava plain deposited by the Pinacate Volcano and dozens of others within the El Pinacate y Gran Desierto de Altar Biosphere Reserve. Then we'd planned to walk part of the Shell Trail across the pink dunes of El Gran Desierto back to the gulf. But now we knew two things: first, after miles of deep, slow sand, salt-laced mud, and stopping to help a Mexican man who had created a roadblock with his stuck car ("I've been stuck three days," he told us in broken English, "way out here lonesome"), we were a full day behind schedule; second, we knew that we didn't know exactly where we were. Because Peacock didn't seem worried, neither were the rest of us. In a way, he had been right when he described how simple the geography was. With the sea to the west and the Pinacate Crater to the north, it was impossible to be lost—but still possible not to have a clue where we were.

Peacock told us that the Shell Trail begins in Ajo and ends somewhere near where we were, at the Gulf of California. Before the time of Christ, young Hohokam men had traveled here from Arizona as a rite of passage. On their way back, they carried shellfish to eat as they walked, dropping the empty shells along the way. Melchior Diaz, an early Spanish explorer looking for the head of the gulf, walked this trail, as did Father Eusebio Francisco Kino, a Jesuit priest who made numerous journeys across northern Mexico in the late seventeenth and early eighteenth centuries. Zoologist William Temple Hornaday and his group followed the trail when they traveled through the area looking for mountain sheep in 1907. Modern desert explorers Bill Broyles and Chuck Bowden followed the trail in the 1980s. In my mind, it was a route paved with shells and packed by generations of human feet.

After three solid days of driving, I got up early and ran west to find the sea. Running there was difficult and slow. The sand was soft, and my path zigzagged in and out of dunes and around clumps of ephedra and seep-willow. I was frustrated by burrows that collapsed under my feet, threatening to break my legs. I stopped ten times in the first twenty minutes to look at piles of shells. There were tracks everywhere—kangaroo rats; lizards; a large bird, probably a heron; and a pinacate beetle, whose tracks looked like stitches holding the desert together. When I got to the ocean, the ocean was gone. I could barely see it disappearing beyond half a mile of mud. I ran back, following my tracks as Peacock had recommended. "Your directions will turn on you out here," he'd said. He was right.

At camp, Peacock was reading a rough draft of his next

book, about his relationship with desert iconoclast Edward Abbey. Bob had found a bone from a heron's wing. It was long, eighteen inches, and jeweled along one side with points where feathers had once been attached. What remained looked like a primitive flute. We loaded the trucks and drove north toward Bahía Adair.

At the end of the road, abandoned tile-roofed villas signaled the bad dreams of a long-gone developer. There we turned west and drove past a large salt pond. We climbed a small hill overlooking a bay that had attracted a thousand birds—herons, curlews, willets, and stilts. Shells were strewn everywhere; surely we had found the end of the Shell Trail.

Evening sun filtered through dreamy clouds, tinting the shells orange. *Chiones.* Winged oysters. Murexes, pink and black. Small cockles. The sacred *Glycimeras cardium,* the size of my heart. ("A great source of mystery and dreams," Peacock said.) And giant whelks, hundreds of them. Standing on that hill, it was a simple journey back to the people whose hands or tongues had touched every one of these shells. Even if I turned a full circle, the world I saw had not changed since a naked Hohokam man had squatted there, pulling meat from a pile of purple murexes he'd gathered that morning. The four of us found a beach below the dunes and set up camp. A million auger shells, like glass drills all pointing east, formed a path to the beach. "I will drive no more forever," Peacock paraphrased Chief Joseph as he threw his truck keys into the sand.

Then Peacock grabbed a shovel and suggested that we walk out onto the mud to find clams for dinner. "Finding the first one is the hard part," he said, not taking his eyes off the mud. He was searching for "active" holes, signs of live clams living below. All around us, curlews knew exactly what they were looking for as they poked their recurved bills into the stiff mud. Suddenly, Peacock stopped and began to dig frantically. "You've got to hurry. They're quick little bastards." I tried to imagine how a clam could be quick, especially when the mud was the consistency of wet cement. The shovel scraped against something hard, and we got down on our knees and dug with our hands, only to find empty shells. We dug four holes before Peacock declared that there were no clams.

Rick and Bob wandered off in one direction and Peacock in the other. I kept looking for clams, convinced that they must be there. In the next two hours, I dug forty holes, dropping to my knees at each one only to find rocks, shells, and more shells. By day's end, I had turned the mudflat into the strafing zone of a major battlefield. At dusk, I staggered into camp with a sore back, elated to have one small clam. Everyone laughed when we saw that what I'd brought back was an empty shell full of sand. We built a fire from an old boat. Instead of fresh clams in our spaghetti sauce, Peacock added Spam.

Coyotes sang and howled all night. In my sleep-altered consciousness, I looked north toward the sounds and saw patterns and colors for each voice, yellow yaps spiraling up from the pups and low, green howls coming in waves from the adults, interrupted by short, high-pitched red spikes. The moon was almost full, and the sounds seemed to be coming from another world. In this desert, the line between dreams and wakefulness was faint.

We spent the next morning exploring the full length of the beach. Following the coyote tracks, we found a dead dolphin two miles from camp. There was no sign of what had killed it— no netting or visible injury. The coyotes had chewed off the tips of its beak, tail, and fins, and an unknown scavenger had broken through its rubbery skin. White vulture shit flowed down the dolphin's side, resembling pictographs.

We drove to Mexico's Pinacate Biosphere Reserve. The brochure offered the following advice: Safety—You're "on your own." Drinking water—"Don't plan on any." Roads—"More roads exist than are on the map. Drivers should be prepared for occasional wrong turns and some difficulty in knowing which way to go." Trails—"There are no trails." There were no crowds there. Had Peacock written the brochure, it would say, "If you get a hole in an oil pan or a shredded tire, or if you lose your car after a hike, you'll be spending the last day of your life sipping urine through lips like charbroiled sausages, trying to keep the ravens from eating your eyes." I liked the brochure's wording better.

The only sign we saw on this trip was a hand-painted one pointing the way to Elegante, a huge crater that had formed some 150,000 years ago. I don't know what I had been expecting, but this crater overwhelmed me. With a diameter of 3,940 feet, it sloped away at a forty-five-degree angle for 300 feet, dropped vertically for many hundreds more, and then curved to a friendly angle toward the bottom. Swifts, like airborne knives, played in the thermals in front of our faces. Then they were gone, and a pair of peregrine falcons appeared so fast that we could hear wings slicing the air as the birds tumbled and swooped, with nothing but play on their minds. We were sure of it.

We camped half a mile down the road. There was no sand, only tiny lava crumbs from Elegante's last eruption. Huge saguaros and paloverde trees made the air seem fresh and green. It was so cool that there, in what was supposed to be stinking hot desert, we felt as if we were stealing something.

Tiny pink flowers (desert sand verbena?) dotted the lava, perfect against the black.

We needed half a day to get back to the border. Bob and I didn't talk much. I realized that I was eager to get home; I thought that Bob and Rick were too. But Peacock was heading back toward the sea, away from home. I worry about him. He's been without a job since Vietnam, with two kids and a wife living hand to mouth on what he writes or what he can borrow. He disappears for weeks at a time and gets into fistfights on the full moon. But out in the wild, Peacock shines. I've learned by watching him that expectations are distractions that obliterate attention. Restoring attention can be healing. Peacock could live in the wild indefinitely, relying on his skills and wits just as our ancestors did for a million years. In Peacock's world, the night sky is a map of where he is, the desert is full of clues about water, a grizzly bear gives signals before charging, and the ocean is a banquet feast. Why can't he function in modern society? Perhaps the problem lies with society, not with Peacock.

Back in Arizona, we turned on the radio to hear some news. The first stories we heard were about a sick woman emitting toxic fumes, sending the people caring for her to the hospital; a young flower girl contracting AIDS at a wedding, where she was raped by the groom; and a religious fanatic gunning down dozens of people who were praying in a holy place. We turned off the radio and thought about Mexico.

We drove through Arizona and into Las Vegas, where the buildings made us feel as if we were dreaming—pyramids, mosques, circus tents. Later, in Utah, we ate dinner at a family restaurant in St. George, where exhausted Mormon parents watched coveys of sticky, same-aged children run wild between the tables. Finally, we fell asleep in the sandstone shadows of Zion Canyon.

Two days later, I was back in my office, the door closed, reading through a stack of library books on Mexico.

Journeys like those made by the Hohokam people to the Gulf of California were more symbolic than utilitarian. Whereas other southwestern cultures made journeys to gather salt and kill eagles, the Hohokam made the shells they carried home into jewelry and amulets. What they were seeking was not just shells and salt but also magic and dream power. They understood the ocean to be the source of rain, and they believed that the wind would blow the rain to their crops only if they made the journey four years in a row. The lives of their people depended on them. They believed that their actions made a difference in their world.

When I asked Gary Paul Nabhan, an expert on southwestern desert cultures, about the Shell Trail, he told me that the people who wandered in the Pinacate region long ago had "song cycles" similar to the "song lines" memorized by Aborigines in Australia—songs that described the mountains and the water to be found throughout the desert. There was a reason why the four of us had rarely known where we were. We didn't know the songs.

We hadn't gone to Mexico to bring back wind and rain or shells. Nothing in our culture required us to go there and look for the Shell Trail, but we went anyway. Science has now explained rain and wind; young men no longer need to walk to the ocean for it. Science has explained away the magic.

Now, for most of us, commercial holidays are all that remain of ancient rituals and meaningful celebrations of life. We are judged by how well we obey the rules rather than by the wind and rain we bring back from the sea.

I thought about the shells I'd brought home—two *Glycimeras* shells, a murex, and three different types of auger—and the bones, a pelican's skull and a vertebra from a dolphin's back. Magic charms? I hoped so. I needed them to be.

A month later, I was wearing down. The happiness and clarity I had found in Mexico were being diluted by noise, like dust forcing its way past sealed windows. Life and death, earth and sky—things that had been in sharp contrast when I got back had begun to mix, turning soft and cloudy. My moods were falling off the scale. I couldn't get away from it.

One night, I dreamed about a dolphin. I was frightened because the dolphin dived deeper than seemed safe. My fear was compounded by a feeling that the dolphin I was watching in my dream was actually me. Even though it needed air, it kept going deeper, where the water got darker and darker. I could feel its chest tighten in my chest. We both needed to breathe. Why didn't it stop? Something was drawing it deeper, something stronger than the need for air. Finally, it reached a sandy bottom. The current had made marks in the sand, and small fish swam about in schools. It was very calm down this deep and almost pitch-black. The dolphin stayed there, his tail barely waving. Then he shot to the surface.

The day after my dolphin dream, I sat down at my desk, and maybe it was the dream's spirit lingering or something else, but the dolphin's vertebra I had picked up in Mexico seemed to glow on my shelf. I closed my office door and picked up that bone. I'd never noticed before how the pad where the disk had once been looked like a face and how the channel for the spinal cord was heart shaped. Then I thought about Mexico, the beach, and the dead dolphin. And the coyotes. How the first night, when they discovered the dolphin carcass, they couldn't really get through its thick, tough skin and had to chew only the parts they could get their mouths around: the fins and the flukes, the dolphin's beak. But the next night—it would have been the night I'd heard the coyotes calling—something else had come by, probably a big raptor with a knifelike beak, and opened up the dolphin's stomach for the coyotes and other, smaller mammals and birds.

I remembered that a man in Puerto Peñasco had told us we might see a dolphin. He had pronounced the word *dolphing,* and I had thought about the fact that in English, *-ing* words are usually verbs, not nouns. With a dolphin, though, that ending would make sense. Dolphins define movement; movement defines dolphins. Dolphin *is* movement. The dead dolphin on the beach didn't make sense. It couldn't have been a dolphin because it didn't move.

I thought back to the first dolphins I had seen in the wild. It was in Glacier Bay, Alaska, and they were surfing the bow wave of our boat. Terry and I were there with her grandparents, Mimi and Jack. Every night, we all went to sleep knowing that Mimi would be asking us about our dreams in the morning. Mimi loved dreams. Her library overflowed with books about the unconscious, about archetypes and dreams. My nights were full of dreams. Mimi said it may have been because we spent all day in nature and that natural objects are archetypes and might affect our unconscious minds. When the dolphins appeared near our boat, Mimi explained that dolphins symbolize playfulness and freedom and joy and that they carry messages between our world and the next. She said that the ancient Greeks saw the dolphin as Poseidon's guide, and Poseidon was god of the sea, which didn't mean much to me at the time.

It was too much. Dolphins surrounded me—in my memory, in my dreams, and on my desk. That night at home, I searched our shelves for books with dolphin references. *Gods in Everyman* by Jean Shinoda Bolen stood out because of its bright cover. My friend Joan had given it to me years before. I opened it to the title page, where she had written a brief inscription: "I found the characters to be most interesting and *recognizable.*" I noticed that below her note, I had written the word *Poseidon.* Then I remembered feeling as if Joan had been trying to tell me something when she gave me the book, something about me being a "Poseidon man." I sat down and read for an hour. Nearly every page was a mirror.

I hadn't thought about Greek gods since elementary school, when I'd learned about each of them and read the stories about who was married to whom and who their children were. We drew pictures of what our favorite god might look like. I drew Hermes because I liked the wings on his feet. Since then, I've learned that the gods can be seen as archetypes of the collective unconscious, the part of the unconscious mind that is shared by every man or woman who has lived.

Reading about Poseidon brought up feelings that had come to me before but never in enough words to verbalize. The Poseidon child is described as a round peg in a square hole, often one who winds up in a family that values manners, rules, and neatness above spontaneity and expressiveness. Growing up in a Mormon family that prized hard work, neatness, and, above all, obedience made life difficult for me. I've had trouble with all these traits. Fortunately, the love we had in my family made that fact less destructive.

I work hard but only on projects I create myself. Neatness has always been fleeting for me, as it is for most Poseidon people. I feel more comfortable in a clutter, and I lose things only when I try to get organized. As a child, I wasn't overtly rebellious, but I always had to think very carefully about obedience to rules.

The Poseidon child, Bolen wrote, is "a fish out of water in the intellectual academic world. He does not set his sights on getting good grades. Academic achievement doesn't hold much meaning for him. And he *usually doesn't know what he wants to be when he grows up* [emphasis mine]."

How long had I been saying that? How many times during long, low stretches of darkness had Terry asked me when I was going to know what to do with my life? I took a deep breath when I read that finding work that matters and succeeding in an "industrial and corporate nation like ours" is difficult for a Poseidon person. Those who do obtain prestige, power, and wealth tend to view their achievements as meaningless. I still get edgy when I talk about the job I left and what I gave up. In our culture, what I did seems ludicrous, irresponsible, and just plain stupid. It is still difficult for me to explain. But for me, quitting my former life worked. And even though I still go through dark periods, they're different now; they're more fertile and quiet times for me to assess which way to move next. I never have the feeling of being glued to time, walled in with no room to move, as I did before.

Poseidon men should work with nature, both wild and human, where "time is measured in cycles, tides, and seasons." In nature, the Poseidon man "learns to trust his instincts and experience with plants, living creatures, currents, weather, or people." Amen.

All the Greek gods have both positive and negative attributes. Poseidon men tend to be emotionally distant, though virtually all American males are discouraged from being emotionally deep or personally expressive. Emotions in males are seen as a sign of weakness. Closing down emotionally is something I do naturally and unconsciously, by default. In the past, when I opened up, Terry, who knows the right questions, was usually responsible. Lately, I feel more comfortable emotionally. I think my dolphin dream helped. The dolphin showed me the way down to a deeper, richer level where emotions are a necessary part of life. I hope I can go there often. Something tells me it takes practice.

Eighteen

MY POSEIDON CHARACTERISTICS of loving nature and trusting my own instincts, combined with the fact that my halflives were drifting further and further apart, made the leap between them downright dangerous. Looking back, I can see that this was especially obvious when I skied.

Since Hink and I first started backcountry skiing in 1972, death has been as much an element of our experience as weather or snow. On our first day, we discovered the excitement of being "out of bounds" in the Wasatch Range, beyond ski area boundaries in places where the possibility of being caught by an avalanche always lurked in our minds, though we never talked about it. We never talked about any danger.

We aren't the only ones who know that skiing untracked powder in the backcountry can be risky. Annual statistics show soaring increases in the number of people searching for skiing's wild essence by trading a lift to the top and the safety of a ski resort for long, hard climbs and a heightened possibility of death. Although most skiers take avalanche safety courses, slides still kill a handful every year.

I have studied avalanches, and the fear from this new knowledge has added an edge to my skiing. I would even say that learning to deal with my fear of avalanches has changed my life. Now, instead of turning away, I'm able to face anything that scares me, even death.

When I'm skiing, I feel something or someone moving alongside me, like a shadow or a spirit my own size, reminding me to stay awake and alert. *Hold the moment; watch.* This presence has never turned on me. Not yet.

In a sense, death is no longer a part of our modern lives; instead, it is something all its own. When death comes—and it always comes—it is a surprise, as if no one had ever experienced before how final and cold it is, how dark and horrible. When death comes, funeral directors are paid to deal with it. They come and take the body away to another place, where they empty it and fill it with chemicals. Then they paint the skin, style the hair, and put the body in a coffin. Later, upstairs, friends and family members walk by the body in its final bed, saying, "Doesn't he look peaceful?"

We were all there in her bedroom the night Terry's mother, Diane Tempest, died of cancer. She was the first dead person I'd seen, other than grandparents in coffins. On the night of Diane's death, I learned that death is not a particular moment but a process. We felt coldness gradually overcome the warmth of her life, beginning with her feet and slowly climbing up through her legs. Near the end, the time between her breaths became so long that the wind on the windows was the only way we knew that time was passing. I am still haunted, seeing her lying there, dead, her body waiting to be taken away while we waited for her next breath.

My own mother spent the last weeks of her life attached to a machine that gave her the breath she couldn't take herself. At age sixty-two, she had gone into the hospital complaining of chest pains and had been told she needed a second coronary bypass. The operation provided new pathways for the blood feeding her heart, but her lungs didn't recover as they had the first time. She developed acute respiratory distress syndrome, or ARDS (also called stiff-lung syndrome, shock lung, or wet lung), as do 2 percent of all coronary bypass patients. This disease is similar to the pulmonary edema afflicting climbers on Mount Everest, where low oxygen concentrations at the high altitude can cause a person's lungs to fill with fluid. Each year, some 150,000 people get ARDS, mostly after severe trauma involving multiple fractures, near drowning, third-degree burns, or transfusions. Most of them die. When it happened to my mother, I was there with my father and all my brothers and sisters. We knew what turning off the machine meant, and I kept thinking we were keeping her from something. Was she aware of us in some otherworldly way that made delaying the end worthwhile and the decision to unplug her from the respirator the hardest thing any of us had ever done? Or was she hoping for an end to her agony?

Regardless of what brings death, why it comes, or how long it takes, there is no leading up to it. With both of our mothers' deaths, Terry and I were on our own. Dealing with the last hours of my mother's life was less daunting and mysterious for me, having gone through it with Diane. But in both cases, nothing in either of our pasts prepared us for what death demanded.

Perhaps I like dangerous sports—climbing into deep sandstone canyons, running wild and alone, skiing steep powder—because when I'm engaged in them, I touch death. In a strange way, tempting fate feels good at a time when death has shriveled and dried and all but disappeared, as gone from our lives as it has ever been in our history. Somehow, and I know it sounds crazy, maybe danger keeps death alive. Without death watching us, we let our attention lapse and death sinks deeper inside.

What happens when we ignore death, forget it, let it dry up inside us, hidden in time? Does it get caught in our veins, clogging and closing down our weakened hearts? Is it the cancer seed against which our handicapped immune systems wither? What if acknowledging death, giving it dignity and power to influence us, helps protect us from the damage we're doing to ourselves with our modern lifestyle? Maybe seeking out danger is less about adventure and more about not waiting around for life to hurt or scare us, but setting up situations to face it head-on, looking life in the eye.

In the canyons, danger comes in the remoteness, the wildness. Southern Utah is popular with tourists, but they don't experience much true wildness. There are literally millions of acres of rock canyons and high plateaus that few people see and nobody really knows. There may still be places no human has ever been.

Finding routes along geologic formations, in and out of streambeds and through cracks in time, is risky. But exploration has large rewards, and the feeling I get from a day of surviving using innate abilities and ancestral skills to find my own way is all I need. Part of the experience is the possibility of falling and breaking an ankle or leg or having an anchor pull out while rappelling into a canyon. Here, unlike the rest of life, there is no place for complacency. I used to dream I was rappelling into a canyon no human had ever been in before and then pulling down the rope only to find that my next obstacle was a waterfall so high that my rope wouldn't reach the bottom. With no way down or back up, my dream was not so much about panic, fear, or dying as about how I would spend my time waiting in the heat, what it would be like to have no choices, and the experiences my mind would go through as it became addled by the inevitable.

When I run, I usually run alone. I never know where I'm going until I get there. Sometimes Terry will call me at work to ask about my plans, and I'll tell her that I need to run and what time I think I'll be home. But I can never tell her where I'll be running because I don't know. When I'm finished at work, I just drive to one of a dozen places in the foothills above Great Salt Lake. When I'm in southern Utah, I'll often stop near an interesting-looking canyon or cliff and go for a fast, hard hike, running part of the way.

This afternoon, I leave a meeting in Escalante and am not scheduled for anything until later in the evening. I drive east a few miles and notice an interesting ridge stretching to the north, so I turn onto a dirt road to get closer. Finding a wide spot, I stop the car and change into shorts and T-shirt, and I'm off. Usually, if my route is straightforward or familiar, I let my mind go. When I do this, I always seem to come back with new ideas or answers to tough questions. Other times, in rough or steep terrain, fear sets in and I focus solely on where I'm going.

Today, east of Escalante, the terrain is easy, but I try to stay on the rocks and not leave tracks. (It's a game I play.) A mile from the car, I think about falling and breaking my leg. I think about how long it will be before someone notices and begins looking for me. I estimate that when I miss the evening meeting, my friend Mark, who will be there, will call my office and get my answering machine. Since Dave, my partner, is out of town, Mark will probably leave a message: "Hey Brooke, did you forget the meeting?"

Terry will begin to worry by the next day because I'd planned on driving home late after the meeting. She will have been expecting a call all day. Still, it will be at least twenty-four hours before she is frantic enough to call Mark. Mark, knowing I'd had the meeting in Escalante, will call someone who was there, ask whether he or she saw me, and find out what time I left. All this time, I will be lying, hurt, in some exposed canyon with just a swallow of water, trying to keep warm. If I am lucky, someone will find my car (it isn't far off the highway) and begin a search. Even though I left very few tracks, they might find me two days later, minimum. I'll be careful. Maybe I'll start leaving tracks.

Most running and canyoneering accidents can be attributed to "player error," or poor judgment; bad luck; or bad weather. One thinks that accidents and freak storms always happen to someone else, somewhere else. Then, suddenly, what a surprise. Avalanches are different: they are always there, alive, waiting in the mountains.

Early one winter morning when it was still dark, I began the Saturday morning ritual: cook oatmeal, dress for skiing, and pack—extra clothing for warmth, water, food and energy bars, first aid supplies, electronic transceiver, and shovel for finding a skier caught in an avalanche. Terry was beginning her part of the ritual. Without getting out of bed, she had called the avalanche forecast center and was relaying to me what she heard. A recording provides updated snow and weather conditions and describes the snowpack and the possibility of avalanches.

"The danger is extreme," she told me; "a good day to ski at a resort." Then she described the reasons, using the terms she had heard, knowing that although they didn't mean much to

her, they would to me—phrases such as *inverted snowpack* and
poor bonding layers. "Why are you going?" she asked, even
though she knew it was because I had to. She also knew that
spending some of her day worrying would be better than spending all of it with me and the dark mood I would be in if I wasn't
skiing.

"Don't jinx me," I said. "There are ways we can go." I was
referring to the fact that even in the worst avalanche conditions,
there are always safe routes—along ridges, through trees.

Another part of the Saturday morning ritual is the kiss. This
is the big kiss, different from the one I get when I leave for
work, because at the back of our minds is the knowledge that
this kiss could be the last.

Before I could kiss her and leave, my mother and her father
called to ask why I would go skiing on a day like that. It is hard
not to be aware of the danger in Salt Lake City, where some
radio stations play more avalanche forecasts than traffic
reports. And when the danger is high, even the morning news
mentions it. "Stay home," my mother said. "Relax; you never
relax."

In a confident voice, Terry told her father that I knew the
safe places, even on a day as dangerous as that.

"Why take a chance?" I'm sure he said, although she kept it
from me.

They are scared because they don't know about avalanches, I
remember thinking.

For them, *fear is ignorance.*

Two hours later, three friends and I are moving like turtles
through a forest of aspens in deep, unconsolidated snow. I have

only a dozen different ski partners and trust them all. I think that picking skiing or climbing or hiking partners is almost as important as choosing who you marry. I need to be with people who I know will be honest with me even when I don't like it, people I can trust when I've lost the ability to trust myself. Beyond that, I need to be with people for whom skiing is just a part of an interesting life. These people trust life and recognize the feeling they get when conditions turn extreme. And I can't stand whiners.

Only one of my regular ski partners is a woman. I feel safe with all my partners, but when I'm with Joan, we seem to pay more attention, not just to danger but also to shadows, animal tracks, and moving clouds. In my observation, men push the limits more than women do and are more likely to let their quest for adventure get them into trouble. Some might blame the gender difference on testosterone poisoning, but I think it has more to do with survival of the species. Wouldn't it make sense that in a group, the men are more expendable than the women in the goal of creating the next generation? Is this why game managers who are trying to build up elk herds allow hunters to kill only bulls? One cow can give birth to only one calf (or two, if she bears twins) no matter how many bulls there are. On the other hand, one bull can feasibly impregnate two dozen females during one rutting season. Why wouldn't this also apply to humans? Did our early ancestors send men out to hunt woolly mammoths because they were more expendable?

Joan doesn't say much when we're skiing. But when she does, I always listen.

It is a bright, fresh day in the Wasatch Range. Today is the first clear break in a stormy week, and I feel as though a dull filter has been stripped from my eyes. Usually, cooling temperatures toward the end of a storm make the new snow lighter than the snow that fell when the storm started. However, the air warmed during the most recent storm, leaving denser snow on top of a feathery layer—"like a Dodge resting on a pile of potato chips," as avalanche forecaster Bruce Tremper described it. These hazardous conditions have made trail breaking almost impossible for us. Instead of staying high in the snowpack, in light snow on top of a dense layer, we sink through the dense layer deep into the feathers.

We break trail, trading leads every fifteen yards, sweating like weight lifters, climbing toward a ridgeline separating Big Cottonwood Canyon from Park City. These mountains are familiar to me, even in areas where I've not been before. I recognize their patterns and characteristics in the same way that, even though I may not always recognize an individual bird, I know its species by its wing or rump patch, the color of its underside, or its flight pattern. In these canyons, trees on the eastern slope differ from those on the northern and northeastern slopes. I've learned how minor ridges rib together with major spines and how wind acts in this place.

We reach the ridge and rest on a perfectly safe horizontal shelf. To the west, a huge cornice hangs out over a forty-degree slope on which an avalanche has already occurred. There is a four-foot crown and fracture at the top, where the snow broke loose, and below that, a white strip mine the size of a football field. None of us speaks, but we are all thinking the same thing.

On a normal day, we would dig a snow pit on the slope to expose the history of that winter's weather and the condition of the snowpack. An experienced skier can feel with her fingers the warm day when the sun turned the top snow layer to mush or the one day it rained, creating a layer of ice. The deep, loose, sugary crystals that form during a temperature gradient meta-morphosis signal danger. A prudent skier will dig out a column at the back of the pit, exposing three sides. The dropping of a shovel blade at the point where the column joins the pit, to test the snow's stability, is called a shear test. A collapsing column indicates a weak layer and higher avalanche potential. Today, we don't need a pit to sense the danger.

In five minutes, we are moving again. Conditions are too dangerous for skiing—there will be no heart-stopping rhythmic dances through waist-deep snow and no breathing between arcs as if our legs controlled our lungs. There will be no playing love games with gravity, none of the motion that we've learned is an invisible part of our lives. We arrive at the top, eat cold bur-ritos, and I wonder what it would be like to ski the long, funnel-shaped chute below us, the way I once wondered about women and what might have been. Then we turn and ski back the way we came.

Two skiers pass us, smiling and thanking us for breaking trail, and continue to the top of the chute, where they stop to put on their jackets. None of us can believe they feel safe enough to ski that chute. We aren't being critical. At least once, beauty or adventure or the combination of both has turned each of us stupid.

For them, *Ignorance is bliss.*

Without warning, the first skier drops into the chute and makes a long, tentative turn. In less than an instant, the slope shatters like a mirror dropped into a sink. Each block of snow begins dropping faster than a free fall, as if powered by some new force stronger than gravity. I don't hear the snow cracking or any rumbling as it falls. Maybe my brain isn't powerful enough to process the intensity of what I am seeing and allow me to hear at the same time.

The slide stops before its image reaches us. We stand there, paralyzed for a moment, and then we scramble to the ridge edge, where we can see the bottom of the slope. The world's luckiest skier lies on his stomach on top of the rubble. His skis are gone. So are his pack, his hat, and one of his gloves. I notice my hand resting on my heart. I'm not sure if it is to pledge some sort of allegiance to what I've witnessed or to grab my electronic transceiver to prepare to search for him. When he moves, we all breathe again. No twisted bones are visible, and no strange noises come from lungs punctured by broken ribs. He rests there, head down, like a modern-day Jonah burped up by a whale.

Ignorance, according to the dictionary, is the condition of being "without education or knowledge." How can this be, when *ignore* means simply to refuse to pay attention?

I'm not sure whether it's proper to use words as factors in mathematical equations, but if *fear is ignorance* and *ignorance is bliss,* then doesn't it make sense that *without ignorance, fear equals bliss*?

I've imagined getting caught in an avalanche, the earth being swept out from under me, being engulfed by a pure white sea, tumbling through space as if the planet had been cut loose from its orbit. If I didn't get strained through trees, flushed over a cliff, or twisted or bent or crushed by the mass of it, I might be one of the 50 percent of avalanche victims who are alive when the slide stops. According to the experts, avalanche debris can transfer oxygen, even though it is nearly impossible to dig through without a stout shovel. Still, I would lose consciousness as the moisture I exhaled froze on contact with the snow all around me, forming a death mask of ice that sealed me off from the outside world. If I'd done everything right (swimming, fighting to stay near the surface, forcing my hand toward the sky, where someone might see it after the slide stopped), and if I'd picked partners who stayed cool and knew how to use their transceivers effectively, I might be dug up before the lack of oxygen turned off my brain and then killed me. People who have lived through this remember a calmness, a euphoric feeling like a soft blanket being pulled around them as they faded beyond consciousness. But this calmness is not what I imagine.

I imagine the panic of being cemented in snow with no way to move. I know this feeling. I have it when I wake up from winter nightmares, struggling, trapped beneath a heavy down comforter weighed down by three fat cats. I imagine horrible dimensions of cold and dark. I might think about hope and how often I'd used it as an excuse for laziness and apathy but how it works for the helpless. I might try to be calm, thinking that calmness could extend what life I had left. Would my life pass before my eyes as if on slides or video? Would it be in color? And what about prayer? (What is the relationship between hope and prayer—aren't they both ways we admit to powerlessness?) Would I worry about Terry, her panic and horror and what she would go through on learning that my death came for me not at the end of a long, fruitful life but in the middle, after my having taunted it?

A few years ago, an experienced skier was killed in an avalanche in the Utah Backcountry, leaving a wife and child when he died. Before then, when I worried about death, my thoughts had been strictly personal: all I would miss, all I wouldn't be able to do with my life. But something about that accident haunted me so much that I wrote the man's wife a letter. I told her I was sorry and how much I liked to ski and how my wife constantly worried when I was out. Then I asked her what it had been like when her husband didn't come home, as Terry always worries I won't.

After I mailed the letter, I felt stupid, thinking I had pried into a dark and private place where I didn't belong. Yet she wrote back: ten pages in beautiful handwriting, not one word crossed out. It was as if she had felt a duty to tell her story so Terry might avoid that same hellish ordeal. Although death may be an interesting journey for the dead, it can be hell for the living.

I photocopied part of one page and had it laminated, and I now carry it like a license in my wallet, a reminder to be careful. This woman's words are with me whenever I go skiing:

> Don't make her have to pray that your body will be found before the next storm drops two more feet. Don't make her have to go to your closet and sniff all your shirts for the strongest-scented clothes for the rescue dogs. Don't make her have to see you with snow packed into your nose and mouth and your arm raised up, frozen solid. Don't make her have to wear that *incredibly strong odor of fear, like a perfume* that she will pick up on her hair and cheek when she kisses you goodbye in the cold back room of the mortuary.

Buried under the snow, I might not think about anything. I hope I would not panic and would try to control my breaths, slow them, but the crush of the snow like a tree or a car on my chest would allow just shallow half or third breaths. Euphoria? No. The first two or three breaths might work. The fourth or fifth would be drastic. By the eighth, I imagine that it wouldn't matter whether my ice mask had formed because my head would be going dark. My last conscious moments would be filled with terror. I know they would.

I tried breathing shallow breaths while sitting by my mother in the hospital as she was dying. Even on the respirator, my mother could only partially fill her lungs. How badly we wanted her to toughen up and breathe on her own without the machine, for us, not for her. "You can do it," we said. "You've got to breathe deeper."

We took turns spending the night with her, dark hours with the machine sucking and sighing and small lights blinking a hellish glow. I was frustrated with her, thinking that if she would only try harder, she could breathe and recover. Then I tried breathing half a breath, as she was forced to do. After less than a minute, I began to feel her terror, gasping, not getting enough air, the pressure building, the beginning of suffocation. What was my mother experiencing after a week of half-breaths, not getting air into most of her lungs? Panic must have cut through her like knives and caused her to suffer and suffer and suffer. Her priorities were clear, and they weren't us, our problems, our wanting her to fix everything before she left. No, her only priority was finding an end to her struggle. She wrote notes telling us to let her die. Finally, we did. After one last procedure failed, we had the nurse turn off the respirator.

A month later, my mother came to me in a dream. In the dream, I was trying to punch in the code on the telephone at the entrance to my parents' gated community when I heard her voice in the receiver. "Mother, is that you? I thought you were dead."

"I am," she answered.

"What is it like?"

"It is definitely nothing to be afraid of. I am in a truly wonderful place, and I wish I could explain it to you," she said, "but I can't."

"Why?" I asked.

"It is so far beyond a living person's ability to imagine and way too complex for words."

"Can I see you?"

"Maybe," she said, her words fading away. "I love you."

"I love you."

Maybe religion exists because we can't really know what will happen next.

I still don't know what to think about death. I trust my dreams for the knowledge light can't give, or won't. I trust my mother's insights from her death as I always trusted them from life. But I still don't know how to live with the possibility of my own death. How do I keep death close without letting it kill me?

Nineteen

I HAVE BEEN HEADED THIS WAY FOR YEARS. I am sitting in a camp chair near the kitchen we built from blue and green tarps, nylon cord, and driftwood on an unnamed beach in the Northwestern Arm of Kenai Fjords National Park in Alaska. It is the fifth day of the trip Hink and I have always talked about, the one neither of us could find time for until his sickness forced him to separate what was important in his life from what was not. This trip is important, not just to Hink but to all of us.

I am reading and making notes and scanning the water with my binoculars. A small fire burns next to me. Annie Hinckley and Diane Frank are below, near the water, leaning against a huge driftwood log with their feet buried in warm sand. They are watching their husbands, Hink and Mike, who are fishing from a kayak 400 yards from shore. Annie doesn't let Hink get far from her sight, knowing what life is like without him. The day before we left Anchorage, she explained it to me. "The first time he lost consciousness, it was horrible," she said. "We had no idea why—we're skiing, he gets a headache, and the next thing we know he is unconscious, and not just for hours but for days—ten days. Nothing anyone can imagine is worse than sitting in a hospital watching someone you love, waiting for them to wake up, wondering if they ever will. Nothing."

Annie told me about her personal search to find the cause, the hours in libraries, all the doctors and clinics and tests, and finally, after another long coma, finding an aggressive young doctor who now thinks that what Hink has is an autoimmune disease, a condition in which the body's immune system turns on the body itself. In Hink's case, specific blood vessels in his brain are being attacked. Neurologists call this rare disease primary angiitis of the central nervous system. Hink calls it SWAG, for scientific wild-assed guess.

Hink is fine. I am sure of it after watching him put together the 300 pieces of his canvas kayak, for the first time in four years, without hesitating.

Yesterday, we paddled ten miles to a place where a tidewater glacier was calving into the ocean. The water was filled with icebergs, many of them bloody with the afterbirth of seals, whose yellow-brown bodies disappeared the moment we noticed them. We beached and pulled our boats a hundred feet off the water, in case a calving iceberg sent a huge wave, and ate lunch. We were finished, stretched out in the sun, when Annie pulled out the chocolate. "I'm a little full. Should we eat this now or wait until we need the energy on the way back?"

"You just don't know what might happen," Hink said. "We should eat the chocolate now."

I am going over notes I've made since the beginning of the trip, and I am surprised to find that a small part of every day has been spent doing tasks. Working. Yes, some of the tasks have been the routine acts of cooking, gathering firewood, and paddling to a small gully to collect water from a dripping snowfield. But there have been other tasks that we've done almost unconsciously, as if in response to an ancient schedule in our cells.

On the first day, after we had set up camp and made ourselves comfortable, someone came up with the idea that putting ice inside the drink bag would keep the contents colder and make drinking easier than pulling the bag in from the ocean every time someone wanted a beer, which is what we were doing. The ice was floating all around us; all we had to do was lasso an iceberg and pull it to shore. This task took two full hours and resulted in the discovery that the tip of an iceberg is impossible to lasso from a kayak. We finally herded it close to shore with two of our kayaks, where it beached when the tide fell.

On the second day, we built a kitchen out of beautiful bleached driftwood poles, a couple of tarps, and yards of cord. This was much more than a shelter. This was a kitchen. We could eat, talk, and read there when the wind came up.

On the third day, my task was to gather net floats and other beach paraphernalia. I found floats that fit into four basic categories: the abundant bun-shaped type, in three colors, white, red, and yellow; the plastic orange spheres with exterior rope-eyes; the rubber inflatables with interior eyes; and the rare and endangered softball-sized glass floats (I found only two). I also collected as many useful ropes and interesting bottles from Japan as I could carry.

On the fourth day, we decided to move camp to the other side of the Northwestern Arm. We must have had good reasons; we just didn't know what they were.

Besides all the work, we have spent the days reading, talking, and exploring the area on foot and in the kayaks, getting to know our home and who we share it with—black bears, sea otters, oystercatchers, ospreys. Bald eagles. The days have fresh, smooth rhythms; events and tasks blend into one another. What needs doing gets done, and night comes at the perfect time.

It has been two years since I quit the plumbing business. Back home in Salt Lake City, I get glimpses of the same natural rhythm I feel here in Alaska, but I wonder whether this seamless life is possible as long as remnants of my former life are still alive in my cells. I think back two weeks to a movie Terry and I saw. *True Lies* is a satirical adventure movie starring Arnold Schwarzenegger. Arnold's character in the movie definitely has halflives. His wife and child think he is a boring computer salesman, but in reality, he is an international spy trying to break up a ring of terrorists who have nuclear weapons. Early in the movie, the terrorists follow Arnold into the men's rest room of a large hotel, where a fight ensues. I was captivated: all the equipment I used to sell is destroyed in that scene.

The first to go is the World A Series hand dryer (with fixed nozzle), which Arnold tears off the wall and crashes against the bad guy's head. I had told countless customers that the A Series was vandal-proof; I also knew there was no way anyone would survive after being bonked by a Series A. They're mostly heavy gauge metal. Arnold then rams the guy's head into the urinal, which I think is a Crane 5-100A. I know from the valve's three-quarter connection and its shape that it is a Sloan Royal 186, which needs only a gallon per flush. But much more water than that douses the terrorist when Arnold pulls the handle. With one terrorist down and another to go, Arnold slips into one of the Sanymetal Academy baked enamel toilet stalls. The second terrorist peppers each stall with machine-gun fire, tearing large holes in the doors and frames—a likely outcome, since the stalls are little more than cardboard between two layers of sixteen-gauge metal. An innocent bystander sits terrified in one of the stalls and trembles as his Bradley 522 double-roll toilet paper holder falls apart before his eyes. Bradley had also furnished a combination paper towel dispenser and waste receptacle (Model 234) and what appears to be a tampon dispenser. Why is there a tampon dispenser in the men's room? But then, it could be one of the new condom dispensers that were coming out just as I was quitting. It was hard to tell. Everything was happening so fast.

Annie notices them first. From my chair, I see her leap to her feet. I grab my binoculars and look out to sea. Hink sits in the bow of his red boat, trying to paddle toward shore. Mike is in the stern, struggling with a bent fishing pole. The kayak is on an awkward course, rocked about by the thrashing of a big fish they have hooked.

I look at Annie on the beach, knowing what she is thinking: that Hink is working hard against the fish and the weight of the kayak and that physical exertion forces large quantities of blood through his brain, putting him at risk of falling into another coma. Diane is excited, knowing how big this fish must be and how happy landing it will make her husband.

I look through my binoculars again. Hink has an intense expression on his face, similar to the one he had during the five hours he sat on the roof of the boat that brought us here from Seward, his wool hat pulled down over his ears in the cold, misty breeze. Whatever Hink's bizarre disease has done to his brain, it also has somehow given him more capacity to absorb his surroundings, his attention creating a force between him and this landscape.

Watching Hink and Mike stirs up a warm, seemingly familiar feeling. Welcoming hunters must be basic to our lives, something implacable yet unexplainable, so clear and basic to our deepest selves that it needs no explanation. Hink and Mike could be coming home with pieces of a woolly mammoth or whale, or a mule deer might hang on a pole supported between their shoulders.

For me, camping is always a good way to sort out the difference between my core and my veneer. By living outside and surviving with a tenth or even a hundredth of the items we insist are necessary and watching our bodies respond to wild places, we get quiet and clear. Waiting for men to come home with meat is that and more.

"Halibut." Hink and Mike have managed to get their boat close enough to shore for us to hear them. "A big one." Hink had told me about halibut, about how no sane fisherman wants a live one in his boat. I can see through my binoculars that Mike's arms are quivering and the fish is still thrashing, dousing the boat with seawater. Hink yells for a rope, and I grab a thick one I'd found on the beach. I carry my kayak out to the water and climb in with the rope. It takes me five minutes to reach them. When I get there, the fish seems quiet. "Don't get too close," Hink says. "Make a loop in the rope, and we'll try and get it on his tail." Mike is almost too tired to talk. I make the loop. "Make a bigger one." I make a bigger loop and put it in the water. Shit—it floats. It is a floating net rope. Hink hands me a sinker from his tackle box, and I tie it on. With some of his last strength,

Mike pulls on the pole, and I see the fish for the first time. It is huge and flat and looks like the bottom of the ocean: brown and lumpy. A halibut does not have a top and a bottom but two huge sides, one white and one dark. A young halibut swims upright, with an eye on each side of its head, as does a normal fish. As it matures, it begins to tilt and one eye migrates to the opposite side. Halibut spend their adult lives lying on their white sides and scanning the ocean for food, their two eyes grotesquely plopped on the side of their heads, as if their creator had been in a hurry.

The fish seems as long as my boat but wider. It is tired and its mouth is open, showing off a hundred teeth like white roofing nails. I hold the rope and Mike passes the pole to Hink, who pulls it through the loop. Then he slowly pulls the fish through the loop, trying not to scare it. After one try, we have the rope around the fish's smallest part, right above its flaring tail. Hink lets the fish float there while I cinch up the loop. "Gently," Hink says. "Gently."

I trade the rope for the pole, and Hink gives it a final tug. The fish reacts violently, thrashing its huge, winglike body and tipping both our boats. Hink gives the fish some slack to get it away from us, and we both hold on to the rope until the fish quiets. I hand the pole back to a grinning Mike. Hink ties the rope to the boat, and we paddle to shore.

Annie and Diane are waiting with Hink's special fillet knife, a plastic bucket for the meat, and the ax. I quickly pull my boat out of the water and grab Hink and Mike's bowline. Hink jumps out in ankle-deep water, and we all tug on the rope to bring the halibut in. When its head breaks the surface, it thrashes two more times, as if it knows the fight is over. Hink takes the ax from Annie, and we all stand back. I wince as he hits the fish with two perfectly placed blows to its head. The fish lies there for a minute and then makes one more giant thrash, trying to break all our legs, but we are ready and stand out of range.

We wait for two full minutes to be sure that the fish is dead. It seems even bigger out of water. Two of us grab the rope and tow it to drier ground. Then we turn it over, revealing its pure white underside. Hink and Mike are both soaking wet and exhausted. "Stay away from those teeth," Hink says. I do.

Diane is five feet, three inches tall. She lies down beside the halibut and we note that five feet, three inches is exactly the fish's length. The tide chart in my pocket has a table for halibut on the back. At that length, our halibut weighs approximately 110 pounds. We hold it up for photographs; it takes three of us because the fish is so cumbersome.

I am sad that the fish is dead.

Wielding his knife and using all his veterinary surgical skills, Hink makes one long cut along the fish's backbone, which seems like a side bone. Then he starts at the head and makes a perfect cut down the center of the white side. He carves around the gills and asks me to hold the piece he is beginning to free with short, quick cuts from the clear, jellylike viscera below. I am holding what will be a twenty-pound slab of meat six inches wide, three inches thick, and four feet long. It is the first of four. It is slippery and heavy, and I can barely hang on to it. Hink cuts with such precision, I swear that if he changed his mind, put the slabs back in place, and sewed them together, the fish would swim again. Part of me wants him to do that. I am the only one there who feels this way; but then, I am the only one who has never eaten fresh halibut.

As he works, Hink points out all the body parts. He opens the stomach and finds large fish bones from recent meals. The kidneys and the dark, plum-sized heart are all enclosed, kitlike, in a sac. He points to some parasite eggs that we need to be careful not to touch.

The four twenty-pound slabs overflow our plastic bucket, and it takes two of us to carry the load back to camp. Hink leaves the halibut's head hooked by the backbone to the tail. The ribs enclose the organs. He moves the carcass down the beach, where the tide will cover it or carry it away.

For the next three hours, we cook and eat. With the sharp knife, we cut one-pound steaks off the slab and cook them one at a time in the frying pan with a little butter, more to keep the meat from sticking than to add flavor. There is no need to add flavor. This is the best meat I've ever tasted.

We laugh and drink. We eat the first of three steaks with a knife and fork and the last with our hands, licking our fingers, dripping juice between our legs and onto the sand. Between mouthfuls of halibut, I share my thoughts on work and the tasks we've instinctively done each day. "Sounds like we need a day off," Hink says.

I sit and stare into the fire, thinking about how I've always liked halibut, the white meat rimmed with a blackish silver border on a shrink-wrapped Styrofoam tray from the grocery store cooler. I almost can't believe that only two hours earlier, I had felt the pull of fish power at the end of my rope, watched the fish being cut and opened, held its organs, and then cooked and eaten it. I feel in my stomach three pounds of its flesh, but I also feel some strange waving sensation that I can't control, a direct transfer of animal power entering my body—not just my stomach but my entire chest.

In four days, the boat from Seward will come to get us. Between now and then, we will paddle and watch sea otters. A huge sea lion, bigger than my boat, will circle me and surface to glare at me, making me feel like prey. We'll make rough driftwood furniture for the kitchen. We'll explore deeper into our forest and find a small lake lined with trees hung with moss, where bears hide. We will eat halibut: halibut and eggs, halibut sandwiches, halibut stew, halibut on a stick. Even then, we'll barely make a dent in our supply, and three of the slabs will go home with Hink and Annie to Anchorage in a cold bucket. The fish's carcass will reappear at every low tide; bald eagles and ravens will be on a large rock waiting for it. I will read two John Grisham novels and take twelve pages of notes. Finally, the boat will come. We will load and board it quickly, and for the next five hours we will watch the late day change the colors of the coastline, the sky, and the rocky little islands covered with bird shit and resting sea lions as we head back to port.

A month later, Hink sent me photographs of us kayaking and struggling to hold up the dead halibut. I called to thank him. "Do you still have some of that halibut left?" I asked.

"Yes," he said. "A lot. But eating it frozen is just not the same."

Twenty

I HAVE A NEW COMPANY NOW called Confluence Associates, a new Dave for a partner, and some solid clients. Dave Nimkin is the perfect partner—he has years of experience in developing small businesses, and he was born with a bleeding heart. We work with rural communities, exploring ideas to show how preserving wild places and natural processes need not conflict with rural economic development. We're not getting rich, but if that had been my original plan, we would have started a business someone else had tried before. It's a great job. It should be; I made it up myself.

I nearly never think about my old life, but occasionally something reminds me of those days. Recently, I was in Tropic, Utah, a small town on the edge of Bryce Canyon National Park, participating in a discussion with rural entrepreneurs. They were interested in attracting tourist dollars with unique natural experiences and locally made products rather than water slides and rubber tomahawks. The meeting was like dozens of business seminars I'd attended in the past, but the products were different. This time, I was listening to businesspeople talk about river trips and log cabin motels, custom-made fly rods and homemade soap, not valves and toilets and water heaters.

Last spring, I found myself once again driving through Salt Lake City, my car loaded with products to deliver. How many times had I delivered parts and catalogs to customers who always seemed to be in a hurry? But this trip was different. Instead of replacement valves and catalogs, my truck was filled with meat. Dave and I had come up with the idea that ranchers in southern Utah might adopt new, low-impact grazing techniques if they knew they could sell meat from their cattle for higher prices. We knew that consumers were already buying beef from cattle that had not been given growth hormones or antibiotics. We knew that people were afraid of mad cow disease and *E. coli* contamination and were concerned about where their meat comes from. We guessed that some would buy beef that they knew had been raised in southern Utah according to range protection criteria. However, our plan would work only if the beef tasted good. So we bought two Angus-Hereford steers and had them hauled to a small, locally owned slaughterhouse and packing company in Gunnison, Utah. There, they were killed and the meat was aged and cut into boneless chuck, lip-on rib eyes, 1 × 1 strip loins, sirloin tips, tenderloins, and hamburger. I spent days on the phone convincing several restaurants and a grocery chain to try the meat, and I made arrangements to deliver a tenderloin to a tasting laboratory at Utah State University. I sold what was left to Robert Redford's chef at his Sundance Resort, to be served at the party for the world premier of the movie *The Horse Whisperer*.

Wherever I took the meat, I left a form for those sampling it to fill out. I asked them to rate the flavor, tenderness, and juiciness on a scale of 1 ("Hated it") to 9 ("Loved it"). Because consumers want to know where their meat comes from, I included the following "beef bio":

This meat came from two Angus steers. They were raised by Curtis Coombs on Anthony Coombs's grazing allotments on Boulder Mountain and near the Circle Cliffs in the northeastern part of Grand Staircase–Escalante National Monument. Four months ago, they were moved to the Coombs corral and grain-fed. On Monday, March 24, weighing almost 1,200 pounds each, they were transported in the back of Curtis's truck to South Sanpete Pack. George Blackburn, the owner, and his sons, Travis and Tyler, slaughter every Wednesday. These two steers were killed on March 25. I'll spare you the details, but I've been assured that their end was quick and humane. They were hung in a cooler and aged until April 13, this last Monday, when they were cut up and packaged. I picked them up Tuesday morning and delivered them. We'd like to know what you think of this meat.

When we handed out the survey at Tony Caputo's Market and Deli in Salt Lake City, Tony, the owner, told us he thought the bio said too much. Still, many people tried the Boulder Beef Special, and everyone liked it. No one got sick. And enough people asked where they could buy the meat—some saying they would pay extra for it—to keep us excited about the project. The next step is to establish criteria and methods that will lead to healthier rangelands. We're getting help with this from people who know what they're doing.

But it wasn't until I walked up to a Salt Lake City architect's office that I realized how small the outward, obvious changes I've made in my life are in comparison to the way I feel inside. As I walked through the door, a strange sensation washed over me, like déjà vu and yet different. I didn't just feel as if I had been there before; I knew it. Seven years earlier, I had been there representing Rex W. Williams & Sons. This time, instead of the latest flush valve, I was there to show a door made from ponderosa pine turned blue by fungus. I wasn't concerned about making quotas or what my commission would be if I made the sale. Instead, I wanted the architect to see how beautiful the door was and how functional, sure to open and close and keep the weather out. But more important, I wanted to tell him the door's story. I wanted him to know that the door had been made by Clark Chappell out of wood cut on Boulder Mountain by Kim Torgerson, both of whom are members of the Southern Utah Forest Products Association. Both men have committed themselves to exploring the use of sustainable practices so that their children and grandchildren will have the forests on Boulder Top and Thousand Lake Mountain to enjoy, hunt, explore, *and* cut far into the future. I told the architect that the door had been made from wood that once would have been considered waste and thrown away or burned. I told him that by using doors like this on his projects, he would be promoting forest health and sustainable communities because the Chappells and Torgersons would make more money on doors and floors and beautiful beams for the ceilings of big homes than they ever had by making rough lumber or cutting firewood. Much more.

The architect liked the story, and he liked the idea that he could make a difference. He bought six doors for an expensive home he was designing. The original plan was to paint them white, but once the doors were installed, the owner thought their natural blue stain was so beautiful that she had the interior decor changed to complement them.

At first, I felt awkward in my new business, realizing that I am still a salesman. But now I know that the work we do doesn't matter as much as the way we do it, for whom, and why.

Twenty-one

I T IS SUMMER, AND I AM SITTING ON THE PORCH of the Moqui Motel in Escalante, trying to cool down after a run through the canyons. I am pulling seeds from my socks and the hairs on my legs, marveling at the way nature has covered some of the seeds with microscopic spikes so that they can attach themselves to passing mammals for dispersal. Others, with feathered wings, are built to ride the air. It is barely July, but every day the temperature reaches 100 degrees Fahrenheit. With the breeze I created by moving my sweat-moistened skin through the stale air, I was cooler running than I am sitting.

An hour ago, while running along a small stream in a narrow canyon formed by walls too far apart to jump across but at one point funneling down to a width I could span with my outstretched arms, I found a deer that had recently died from a fall. He must have seen the water from the canyon's rim, miscalculated the rocks' angle or the effect the morning dew might have on his traction, and slipped. I found him lying face-up, staring wide-eyed from the bottom of a two-foot-deep pool of water through the darkness of the canyon to the brilliant sky above. The peaceful look on the deer's face surprised me, and I thought how nice it must be to gaze up through eternity, open-ended time, rather than down into a narrow hole.

I have been in Escalante for two days, attending meetings to discuss ways to diversify the economies of these rural towns. I try to be sure that my work allows me to spend at least an hour or two in the canyons every day so that I am reminded again and again of the importance of protecting wildness in any form. I believe that if humans are to survive as a species, if our world is to last here on earth, it will have nothing to do with what we've invented, developed, and manufactured but everything to do with what we know in our deep cores about being good mammals. Like grizzly bears, slime molds, mosquitoes, and goshawks, we have not been genetically manipulated and we are still wild creatures. We need to act more that way.

But recognizing our ancient ties is difficult when our modern world seems determined to keep its distance from the earth by distracting us into believing that we have gained some elevated stature, that we are better than everything else. In reality, aren't we only engaged in meaningless mitigation for all we lost or threw away when we cut line with nature and most natural processes? As individuals, we are not immortal. As evolutionary creatures, we are. We can live forever as specks in the cells of other beings.

When I am outside, I know the rules, the old rules. I have not memorized them; I have not learned them by having them drilled into my brain year after year; nor did I ever write them one hundred times on my first-grade blackboard when I broke them. I have always known them. The rules for living are in my bones; I feel them. They are simple. I need to eat and drink. My body knows exactly how much. I know how warm I need to stay in winter and how cool in summer. I need to keep track of the weather. I know what can kill me. I was afraid of snakes before I knew what they were capable of; we all were. My body knows that if I survive, my species survives. If I don't, and my death has something to do with weakness or my body's not having known the rules well enough, perhaps my species is better off without me. I'm comfortable with that. Part of me thinks that the deer in the pool had a peaceful look in death because he knew he was somehow making a positive contribution to the survival of his species.

I still have two halflives. On good days, they are so tightly joined that it is hard to tell the difference between them. When I feel divided, I blame the split on lack of attention or discipline, and I know I can refocus on wildness and the survival of our species. My goal is to merge my halflives into one whole life and to die looking out the big end of the canyon toward infinite possibility, not down into a dark pool.

In a moment, I will take a shower and then drive home to Salt Lake City. Tonight, I will take Terry to dinner at our favorite restaurant, where halibut will be the evening's special, served blackened, grilled, and baked. I will order trout because I can no longer eat halibut without first feeling the source and the pull of its strength and life against me.

In what may be the most important thing I do all day, I take the seeds I've pulled from my socks and my legs and toss them high in the air. They are caught in a quick breeze and gone.